"J.D. Greear is a faithful pastor with a bold vision of [ ] cifically Muslims—with the gospel of Jesus Christ. [ ] is insightful and the clarity of his gospel witness shines through."

—**Dr. R. Albert Mohler Jr.**
President of The Southern Baptist Theological Seminary,
host of *The Albert Mohler Program* on national radio and Internet,
and author of numerous books

"A refreshing new approach anchored solidly in biblical truth, free from the excesses and inadequately contemplated claims of a good many contemporary approaches... Both theologically and evangelistically encouraging."

—**Paige Patterson,** President,
Southwestern Baptist Theological Seminary
Former President, Southern Baptist Convention

"There is no book that exceeds this one in terms of theological depth wedded to practical savvy."

—**Dr. Bruce Ashford,**
Director of the Center for Great Commission Studies
at Southeastern Baptist Theological Seminary

"Your book...has helped me communicate much more effectively with Muslims who are seeking the Truth. Now, rather than arguing with my Muslim friends, I end up sharing with them at deeper levels with words and ideas that they can understand."

—**Patrick F.,** missionary to Afghanistan

"The hard work of engaging Muslims, gaining insight into their mind-set and heart-felt spiritual quest, then applying...Scripture to their needs is evident throughout this book...Valuable reading for those engaging Muslims in a variety of settings."

—**Keith Eitel,** Director of Missions
at Southwestern Baptist Theological Seminary

"Rarely have I been so moved by the clarity, freshness, and effectiveness of any con-tribution...to reaching our world in our time...This...approach trumps any I have seen on the bottom line, which is actually *reaching* Muslims with the gospel."

—**Alvin Reid,** Bailey Smith Chair of Evangelism,
Southeastern Baptist Theological Seminary,
and author of *Inside the Mind of the Radically Unchurched*

"This book has profound and captivating insights into Islam that will catapult readers into deeper understanding and better relations with Muslims."

—**Dr. Bruce Sidebotham**
Reserve Army Chaplain
and Director of Operation Reveille

"Very readable and practical...a good introduction to reaching Muslims, and at the same so full of gems that many experienced field missionaries will profit from reading the approaches and ideas presented."

—**Dave C.**
regional leader for Pioneers mission
agency in Southeast Asia

"A tremendous book...It uses very plain language and examples with which students could educate themselves in order to make a difference in their relationships with Islamic students. I would highly recommend this to my students."

—**Miles O'Neill**
Director, Campus Crusade for Christ,
UNC Chapel Hill

"Incorporates both a thorough understanding of the Muslim worldview and practical approaches that explain the Bible in a way that does not clash with that worldview...An approach that is theologically accurate...practical, and culturally appropriate...I endorse this work."

—**Guy Armstrong**
Southeast Regional Director,
Campus Crusade for Christ

"Practical advice for engaging the Islamic culture in conversations of the cross. My time studying Islam...would have had minuscule effect with my Muslim friends had it not been for the guidance...in this book. Thank you for this wonderful tool!"

—**Lance Michels,** seminary student
and missionary to Southeast Asia

# Breaking the
# Islam
# Code

# J.D. Greear

HARVEST HOUSE PUBLISHERS
EUGENE, OREGON

*Cover by Left Coast Design, Portland, Oregon*

*Cover photos © iStockphoto / Distinctiveimages; Cokeker / Shutterstock;*
*Backcover author photo by Kimberly Goodson Naranjo*

**BREAKING THE ISLAM CODE**
Copyright © 2010 by J.D. Greear
Published by Harvest House Publishers
Eugene, Oregon 97402
www.harvesthousepublishers.com

Library of Congress Cataloging-in-Publication Data
    Greear, J. D., 1973-
    Breaking the Islam code / J.D. Greear.
        p. cm.
    ISBN 978-0-7369-2638-6 (pbk.)
    ISBN 978-0-7369-4467-0 (eBook)
    1. Missions to Muslims. 2. Islam—Relations—Christianity. 3. Christianity and other religions—Islam. 4. Islam—Essence, genius, nature. I. Title
    BV2625.G74 2010
    248'.5088297—dc22

                                                            2009021815

**Printed in the United States of America**

12  13  14  15  16  17  18  / VP-SK / 10  9  8  7  6  5  4  3  2

*To the fame of God our Savior among Muslims.*

*To my mom and dad—thank you for preaching Jesus to me in word and deed.*

*To Drs. Paige Patterson and Keith Eitel, who taught me to believe God for the salvation of the Islamic world.*

*And to my precious children—
thank God someone told our family about Jesus!
Kharis, Alethia, and Ryah, your names mean
"Grace" (Greek), "Truth" (Greek),
and "Joyous Celebration" (Malay).
Adoniram, you are named after the first
American missionary to go overseas, the courageous
Adoniram Judson, whose work in Burma paved
the way for thousands of missionaries to follow.*

*May God enable you to take the grace and truth
of Jesus to the Muslims of the unreached world for
their everlasting joy and His eternal glory.*

# Contents

Prologue

# A Story of Friendship

I'll never forget the last day I lived in a Muslim country.

I had spent the morning doing the final preparations to leave the place and the people I had learned to love, so I could come back to finish my schooling in the United States. It was a sad day.

Around noon, a close friend, Ahmed, came over to visit me. He had been one of my closest friends for the last two years. He had befriended me at a time in my life when I was alone in a strange country. We had talked, traveled, studied, and fished together.

I had tried a number of times to bring up Jesus to him, but Ahmed, though always polite, seemed eager to leave the subject alone. He was as committed a Muslim as I had ever met. He was kind of like an Islamic youth pastor, volunteering his afternoons to serve and love underprivileged Muslim youth. When I would talk about Jesus, he would smile and say, "You are a good man of faith. You were born in a Christian country and you honor the faith of your parents. I was born in Muslim country and I honor the faith of mine. You were born a Christian and will die a Christian. I was born a Muslim and I will die a Muslim."

Before I left, I knew I had to have one final conversation with him. How could I call him my friend and not make clear to him what I believed about Jesus Christ?

I met with him about a week before my final day in his country. I told him that, according to the Bible, only those who have believed on Jesus Christ for the forgiveness of their sins can enter God's kingdom. For about 15 minutes he sat politely and listened as I poured my heart out to him. When I was finished, he thanked me for my friendship and left.

I did not see Ahmed again until that last day—the day I was preparing to return home. When he showed up that day at noon, I could tell something was on his mind, so I asked him about it.

"Our conversation," he said. "After we talked the other day, I thought about how much I appreciated you for telling me so directly what you believed. But then I didn't think much of it...*You are a Christian, I am a Muslim*, I thought. *That is how each of us was born, and that is how it always will be.*

"But that night after our conversation I had a dream." He interrupted himself to say, "At first I thought it was one of those dreams that comes from eating strange fish. But I've had those kinds of dreams. This was different... In my 'dream,' I was standing on earth and suddenly, open before my feet, was the 'straight and narrow way' leading to heaven."

---

He then looked at me and said, "What do you think my dream means?"

---

"And as I looked up along this pathway to heaven," he said, "*you* were on it! You arrived at heaven's gates, but the way inside was blocked by huge, brass doors. I thought to myself, *That is where his journey ends. Who has the power to open those doors?* But then, to my surprise, someone inside knew you, and they called your name. The doors then swung open wide for you, and you went in...and then my heart broke because I really wanted to go with you. But then, the doors opened again and you came back out, walked back down the path and reached your hand out to me. And you pulled me up to heaven with you."

He then looked at me and said, "What do you think my dream means?"

Now, understand that I was raised in a traditional Baptist home. Dreams were not a part of our standard religious repertoire. But, not knowing what else to do, I said, "Brother...you are so in luck. Dream interpretation is my spiritual gift!"

For the next hour I walked him through Romans and Acts, showing him how Jesus had come to earth, lived the life we were supposed to live, died the death we were condemned to die, risen again, and now offered salvation to all who would believe.

I would love to tell you that Ahmed became a believer. Sadly, he did not and, to my knowledge, he has not. I think it was still just too much for him.

But what he said next is something I can never, ever forget. He said, "I *know* why Allah gave me that dream. He was telling me that you were sent here by God to show me the path that leads to heaven. You were to teach me God's ways and explain to me his *Injil* [gospel]. But today, my friend, you are going home, and we will probably never see each other again. You are the only Christian I know. Now who will teach me the ways of God?"

I am writing this book in response to that question.

The fact that you are reading even this prologue is an answer to prayer. You may have picked this book up because you have become friends with a Muslim and you want to talk to him or her about Jesus, but you don't quite know where to start. Maybe you are preparing to live in a Muslim community and you want to understand how you can best live out Jesus in front of them. Maybe you have picked it up because you feel a strange tugging in your heart whenever you hear about the Muslim world. Maybe you just want to understand.

Whoever you are, I am grateful you are holding this volume in your hand. You are an answer to prayer. Most of the 1.9 billion "Ahmeds" in the world will never meet a genuine Christian. Muslim college students studying abroad in the United States will never, almost without exception, step foot inside of a Christian home while they are in America. Though over one-third of all the unbelievers in the world are Muslims, only .05 percent of all the Christian workers in the world have Muslims as their focus. Most Muslims, like my friend Ahmed, will die without ever having had someone explain the gospel to them.

For the Muslim you know, you are probably the only Christian they will *ever* know. I hope this book will help you present Jesus to them well.

Ahmed and I corresponded several times after I left, but I lost contact with him after many of his family died in the Southeast Asian tsunami of

2004 and he was displaced to a refugee camp. I know he is still alive, but have not yet been able to locate him. I trust, by God's grace, that one day I will. Ahmed, my friend, this book is for you. I hope we find you.

We have to. We are your only hope.

# Getting to the Issues of the Heart

This book is for those of you who would really like to see a Muslim brought to faith in Jesus Christ but don't know exactly how to make that happen.

In some ways, Muslims can be the easiest people in the world to share the gospel with and, in other ways, the most difficult. *Beginning* the conversation is usually easy because religion is central to Muslims' lives. Unlike Westerners, they are almost always ready to talk about religion. Furthermore, because they share a common religious "heritage" (one God, revealed through the prophets, and so on) with Christians, there's a lot of common ground to get the discussion started.

On the other hand, actually sharing the gospel with them in a way that convinces, or even engages, them is difficult. For all the similarities Islam has with Christianity, Muslims reject outright the most central Christian claims about God: his nature, how we are to be saved, and what he expects of us. Islam is a religion designed specifically to refute (or "correct") Christianity.

Furthermore, the Muslim worldview leads Muslims to ask different questions about God then most religious Westerners do. I often found that the way I was sharing the gospel was not only objectionable to my Muslim friends, but also irrelevant! I was attempting to answer questions they had no interest in asking. Furthermore, there is an extreme distrust existing between Muslims and Christians that arises from misunderstanding of what the other one actually believes, heightened by political tensions around the world.

This book can help you begin to overcome these communication barriers.

It can help you understand how Muslims think, discern what questions they are actually asking about God, and see how the gospel gives the only real answers to those questions.

I have been friends with Muslims for many years. I spent two years living in the home of the sharia law director for a conservative Islamic province in Southeast Asia. I became a part of their family, and they became some of my best friends.

I am less concerned with Islam as a geopolitical movement and more concerned with Muslims as individuals. There are many great and necessary works that discuss the Islamic religion as a dangerous political force, and many others that show the apologetic shortcomings of theological Islam. You have probably heard of or read some of these books.

But I am primarily concerned with Muslims as individuals...individuals Jesus died for and whom he longs to rescue back to himself. If you want to understand Muslims as *people*—how they think, what they care about, and what obstacles you have to overcome to win them to Christ—then you're one of those readers I've written this book for.

In other words, this book is less about winning arguments and more about winning the hearts of Muslims.

## The Quest for Salvation

I want to help you discover the *soul* questions that Muslims are asking about God and salvation. The Bible teaches us that every person, including Muslims, is aware of, in some way or another, their separation from their Creator, and all humans, whether they are aware of it or not, search for salvation. King Solomon tells us that God has planted "eternity" in our hearts, and that sense of eternity gives rise to questions that only he can answer.[1] The apostle Paul said that God had made himself known to us by writing himself into the creation and into the yearnings of our hearts. We may not know we were designed for God, but there is a part of us that yearns for what only a relationship with him will satisfy. As Augustine, the great Christian theologian, said, "Our hearts will always be restless until they find their rest in you."

The human quest for salvation is about more than bliss in the afterlife. The result of our separation from God is a feeling of nakedness and shame before God—the feeling that we are exposed, rejected, and guilty. Just as Adam and Eve first did, we search for a covering—a "salvation" that will take away our sense of shame, rejection, and alienation; a salvation that will give us comfort in this life and safety for the next.

Muslims, like all fallen sinners, usually do not understand exactly what they are searching for, or why what they seek in Islam can never satisfy their deepest longings. Understanding how Islam both acknowledges and attempts to address our distance from God will be the key, I believe, to showing Muslims how the gospel provides the answers to the questions God has placed in their hearts.

Having lived in a Muslim context and studied Islam for years, my conclusion is that the approach that most Western Christians take to sharing the gospel with Muslims does not connect with them. Most Christians explain the gospel in a way that (to use a cliché) "answers questions they have not been asking." This book will help you see what questions Muslims *are* asking, and how the gospel provides a unique and satisfying answer to them.

## God Is at Work

The stark reality we must face is that there has been no mass movement of Muslims to Christ ever in history. It's not that Christian missions to Muslims have been entirely without fruit, just that the vast hegemony that Islam maintains over the Middle East and much of Asia has gone virtually unchallenged. Muslims still, for the eleventh century in a row, make up the majority of lost people on the planet.

> The stars of the sky are my nightly reminder
> that God will bring multitudes of peoples
> from Muslim nations into his family.

Believe it or not, there is a ray of hope even in that dark truth. If the Bible is true, history cannot end without first seeing a movement of the peoples now living in Islamic lands to the gospel. It is only when the gospel has been preached on, and believed by, all nations that the "end" can come (Matthew 24:14). Paige Patterson, former president of the Southern Baptist Convention, once said to me,

> I believe that before Jesus returns we will see a massive turning of
> Muslims to Christ. As I look down through Christian history, I
> see that God has established the superiority of His gospel over all

its enemies. The Roman Empire, once the chief persecutor of the Christian faith, crumbled, leaving Christianity established in its wake. The Roman Catholic Church, which for many years impeded the preaching of the gospel, could not restrain the massive Reformation that spread the gospel throughout the world. In our own generation we have seen the Communist bloc crumble, loosening its chokehold over the church in Slavic and Asian lands. Now we are seeing the greatest movement toward Christ in history among the Chinese and Korean people.

The one great obstacle which the gospel has yet to overcome is the Islamic empire. Small pockets of revival have broken out here and there, but never a sweeping awakening. I believe that sometime soon we will see it. I don't know how or where it will happen. Perhaps it will be the result of a change in methodology. But it will be a mighty outpouring, and I believe Muslims by the thousands will come to Christ. It is consistent with how God has worked historically in the world.[2]

I cannot wait for that day. I live in daily expectation of its arrival. Until it happens, I have resolved to labor, believe, and wait for the salvation of Muslims. The stars of the sky are my nightly reminder that God will bring multitudes of peoples from Muslim nations into his family (Genesis 15:5). Some of the stars Abraham saw were for the Muslim peoples living today! For now, I want to be like that proverbial woodpecker pecking away at the telephone pole when lightning strikes the pole and splits it in two. When that happens, I will pull back, undoubtedly shocked and a little dazed at what just happened, but not really surprised. I knew it would come. God told us it will come. I believe him. I hope this book will entice you to join me.

## Where We're Headed

Here is how this book will flow.

The first four chapters will help you get familiar with who Muslims are, how they think, and what is important to them, so you can know how to talk with them in a way that connects with them. In chapter 1 we'll discuss how to create the right environment for a conversation about God; in chapter 2 we'll analyze what moves and motivates Muslims; in chapter 3 I'll give you a brief overview of what Muslims believe; and in chapter 4, we'll discuss a lot of the misconceptions we have about Muslims and that Muslims have about us.

In chapter 5, "The Muslim Salvation Code," we'll get into their theology and culture and identify the "questions" they are asking about God and salvation. In this chapter I'll help you see how the soil of the Muslim heart has been uniquely prepared for the gospel. Chapter 6, "Re-coding the Gospel," will help you present the gospel in a way that answers those questions.

In chapter 7, "The Gospel Confronts the Ultimate Religion of Works," I'm going to show you how Islam is, at its core, a religion of "works-righteousness." I'll show you how much of Jesus' teaching in the gospels is directed at religious systems of works-righteousness, like Islam. We'll look at what Jesus said and how he said it, and think about how to apply it to the works-righteousness of Muslims.

In chapters 8 and 9, we'll take a brief look at the primary objections that Muslims bring up whenever the gospel is presented. My goal in these chapters is not to address every Muslim objection to Christianity. My goal is to explain how you can turn many of the *primary* Muslim objections into *opportunities* to share the gospel. My goal is to help you keep the conversation on track and not get sidelined in arguments that lead nowhere profitable.

In chapter 10, "The Challenge and the Hope," I'll conclude the book by considering what Jesus says is required of us, his witnesses, if we are to see Muslims come to Christ. I hope you'll see that the fields really are white for harvest, that God is willing and able to save, and that all that is necessary now for the salvation of Muslims is a team of committed, believing laborers in their fields.

I've included a couple of additional resources at the end that I believe you'll find helpful. This first is a collection of references to articles, books, and Web sites that can take you deeper into some of the issues we don't have time to get into thoroughly in this book. There's a lot of helpful (and some unhelpful) literature out there, and I hope this will help you wade through it.

The second is called, "Speaking in Islam Code: How Far Is Too Far?" We'll look at a rather controversial issue called *contextualization*. How far can we go in "encoding" the gospel in Muslim terms before we compromise the heart of the gospel itself? This is one of the most difficult theological questions Christians sharing Christ with Muslims face. If you go too far in

"Islamicizing" the gospel, you'll distort the message—but if you don't go far enough, you'll obscure it!

This will be, I believe, an exciting journey. There are few things as exhilarating as seeing a Muslim come to Christ. At times, however, this task seems impossible. Maybe you are there now. Maybe you've hit a wall in sharing Christ with a Muslim friend and you don't know how to get around it.

The good news is, we serve a God who delights in doing impossible things. He called light out of darkness, and told dead men to get up out of their graves. *That* God has promised to help us in this journey. In fact, he promised that if we would follow him *he* would teach us to be effective "fishers of men."

So, why not begin right now by asking him to teach you his ways as you dive into the pages ahead?

# 1

# Creating an Environment
# for Conversation

I used to think that the most effective way to share Christ with Muslims was to prove to them that Christianity was right and Islam was wrong. I thought that if I showed Muslims all the holes in Islamic logic, the factual inaccuracies of the Qur'an, the violent history of Muslims, and the superiority of Christian truth claims, they would become Christians. Overwhelmed by the force of my logic, they would rush to Christ. So I studied diligently.

My study paid off, at least in one sense. I won lots of arguments. Unfortunately, I won no Muslims to Christ.

That is because the roots of Muslim beliefs are not found in their minds, but in their hearts. Most Muslims do not choose to believe in Islam because they have carefully studied the facts and become convinced Islam is the best explanation. They believe it because they are raised in it. It is part of who they are. They *want* to believe it.

This is true for almost all of us. Our "hearts" (that is, our desires, viewpoints) shape how we see things and determine what makes sense to us and what we accept as true. We are not unbiased, calculating reasoning machines. As the philosopher Blaise Pascal said, "The heart has its reasons which reason knows nothing of." Or, in the postmodern words of nineteenth-century philosopher William James, we believe what we believe because we have the "will to believe" it.

Believing certain things makes our lives easier, helps strengthen family ties, and gives us security for the future. That is often *why* we choose to believe them. Few of us, if any, believe what we believe solely on the basis of "pure reason," even if we think we do.

The apostle Paul explained centuries before Blaise Pascal or William James that our primary problem with knowing God is not that we are ignorant of truth but that our sinful, dark hearts have suppressed the truth that we do grasp. God has revealed his truth all around us—we simply do not want to see it (that is, until God creates a desire in us to see it—Romans 1:18-21; see John 7:17 and 1 Corinthians 2:14-16).

## A Message for the Heart

Your message cannot be simply a defense of Christianity and an attack on Islamic beliefs. You have to get beyond Muslims' minds into their souls. You not only have to understand what they believe but *why* they believe it. You have to understand what is important to them, what disappointments they find in Islam, and what questions they are still asking about God. This will mean three things for you as you attempt to share Christ with the Muslim.

First, *you can most effectively share Christ with Muslims when you are genuinely friends with them.* Life on life is as important with the Muslim as mind on mind. Because the decision to trust in Christ is a *soul* decision, not just a *mind* one, it will most likely not be arrived at in the heat of debate. We have to show, in a way Muslims can see and understand, that Jesus is better than anything else they hold on to for security, and that he is the treasure worth selling the "field" of their lives to obtain (Matthew 13:44). Like Christ, we must "incarnate" ourselves in the lives of Muslims and show them his love and joy in the context of friendship. Christ did not shout at us from heaven, leave gospel tracts on our porches, or broadcast his message in from heaven via radio. He came to live among us. He served us. He lived out the love and joy of God in front of our eyes. We "looked upon" him, and our "hands handled" him (see 1 John 1:1-2).

Second, *you must learn to listen to Muslims.* Listening is how you will discover what is going on in their hearts, what is important to them, and where God is already at work in them. As I will try to show you in this book, God has already planted questions in their heart. Once you learn what you're listening for, you'll see they are asking them over and over and over.

As you listen, you will learn how to craft the gospel message in a way they can understand it. We must be people of "double listening." We must listen to God's unchanging message on one hand and the hearts of our Muslim friends on the other. Only then will we be able to craft the gospel message in a way that Muslims can understand it. This is partially what made the apostle Paul so effective. As he explains in Galatians 2:7, Peter preached a "gospel for the circumcised" (the Jew) and Paul preached a "gospel for the uncircumcised" (the non-Jew). This does not mean that there were two different gospels—Paul and Peter are clear that there is only one way for all people to be saved! (See Peter's words in Acts 4:12 and Paul's in Galatians 1:8.) Rather, it means that the one gospel can be expressed in different ways that will connect better with the people who are hearing it.

Listening is also how you will establish trust. As M. Scott Peck famously said in *The Road Less Traveled*, "To listen to someone is to love them." Listening, and understanding, is the core of friendship.

You and I often think of our role as Christians as explaining a message. But it is listening that makes our explaining effective! Listening establishes trust, and listening helps us make our message understandable.

Third, *you must look for the Holy Spirit to do in the heart of your Muslim friends what you cannot do.* Only the Holy Spirit can make blind eyes see; only he can make the gospel make sense to a Muslim. It is not some new insight you have or new angle I give you on sharing the gospel that will magically unlock your Muslim friend's heart. The human heart, until God opens it, is hardened against him, darkened in its understanding, and does not even know to ask the right questions about God! In what theologians call our "natural" state, the gospel seems like foolishness to us! It takes the illumination of God's Spirit and his regenerative work inside our hearts before we will ever believe.[3]

God himself has to plant the right questions within us and make us open to the answers. This is not the result of a new technique, but of a miracle that God does in us. The only thing you can do is faithfully explain the message, pray, and trust in God to awaken the heart.

## Three Preliminary Questions

As you seek to really understand and befriend Muslims, there are three questions you should constantly be asking. These are the questions that true friendship and genuine understanding are built upon. In many ways, these three questions guide the thought of the rest of this book.

The first is, "*What does my friend actually believe?*" We'll get into what

Muslims formally believe in chapter 2. Beyond that, however, most Muslims actually buy into a number of unorthodox beliefs (such as animistic or superstitious practices) that help them relate God to their day-to-day lives. It is essential to understand these unorthodox dimensions of their lives if you want to share Christ effectively with them.

---

Psalm 19:4-6 declares that there are no people anywhere who have not heard the voice of divine truth.

---

These practices often reveal a question God has implanted in their hearts that Islam has not satisfactorily answered. Missionary Don Richardson once noted that God has left in the cultures of all peoples certain "redemptive analogies" that prepare them to receive the gospel. After years of failed attempts to explain the gospel to the Sawi people of New Guinea, Richardson discovered an ancient custom, the "peace child," that gave a perfect picture of what the gospel was. In Sawi culture, when two tribes were at war and wanted to come to terms of peace, a child from one tribe was exchanged for one from the other tribe. Each would grow up in the opposing tribe. As long as the child from one tribe was alive and well in the other tribe, the two tribes remained at peace. Using this "redemptive analogy," Richardson explained to the Sawi how God had given his own peace child to men. His presence in our flesh guaranteed his continued favor on us.[4]

So, knowing what an individual Muslim actually believes—both in their "creed" and in their day-to-day practice—will help us see places where the gospel can speak to heart issues.

The second question is, *"Why does he believe that?"* Understanding the reasons *why* the Muslim believes as he does is as important as understanding *what* he believes. Understanding "why" reveals the "question behind the question"—that is, the soul question that must be addressed. When all the smokescreens have been cleared, what is it that keeps a Muslim within the Islamic faith? Is it fear? Tradition? Ignorance? Fear of rejection by others? To show how Christ is worth the losses that will come with becoming his follower, we have to understand what those losses will be! We have to show that Christ is better than all that the Muslim holds on to for life and security.

The third question you should be trying to answer when you're befriending a Muslim is, *"Which of his beliefs, questions, and experiences can I affirm?"*

Starting with the legitimacy of his questions is the best place to begin dialogue. Romans 1:18-21 explains that all people have perceived divine truth from creation and from their conscience.[3] Psalm 19:4-6 declares that there are no people anywhere who have not heard the voice of divine truth. Jesus told us that the fields were already "white for harvest." In other words, the Holy Spirit is working pre-conversion to bring individuals to Christ. We should try to discover where he has already been at work in the Muslim's heart.

Identifying what Muslims believe about salvation and how we can use those things to point them to Christ will be the subject of the next four chapters. But before we get there, let's take a look first at how Muslims try to convert others. How they attempt to convert others provides a window into what they value in their religious experience.

2

# Understanding What Moves the Muslim

In this chapter I want to show you what moves—motivates—the Muslim by discussing the ways that Muslims usually try to convert Christians to Islam. This will show you what is important to Muslims about their religion—what they find most attractive, and what they think you will be moved by as well. Then we'll look at what Islamic converts to Christianity usually say was their primary motivation in converting. Not surprisingly, it was the same three things Muslims used to try to convert me that Muslim converts most often identify as instrumental in their coming to Jesus.

## How Muslims Try to Convert Christians to Islam

I was the special conversion project of an entire Muslim village. Since I was one of the first and only Westerners in the area, local Muslims told me I had been sent to them by Allah so they could educate me in the ways of Islam and show me its superiority, and so I could convert to Islam and take the message back to my people. They used, primarily, three things to try to convince me.

### The Beauty of the Qur'an

First, they wanted to expose me to the beauties of the Qur'an in its original Arabic. More than once, visitors in my home asked if they could read to me from the "beautiful al-Qur'an." They would not read it to me in English, nor even in their own tongue. They insisted on reading it to me in

Arabic. Most had never read it in their own language, and most had little grasp of the content of its teaching.

The Qur'an is hard to read as "literature." It contains no plot, does not tell stories, and does not substantially argue points. Its chapters, called *suras*, are arranged from longest to shortest (with the exception of the first introductory sura). The Qur'an reads like a seemingly random compilation of splintered revelations and exclamations given with no historical context. The power Muslims accord to the Qur'an is not in its teachings, but in its *hearing*.

Muslims believe the Qur'an, in its original Arabic, has a magical power on the soul, even if heard without understanding. This, I learned, was one of the reasons they insisted on blasting the call to prayer (*azzan*) over the loudspeaker (located, unfortunately, not far from my window) five times a day. Not only is it the call to prayer, it is the dissemination of the word of Allah, giving Allah's word opportunity to work its mysterious power in the ears of its hearers. The more I got exposed to the sound of the Qur'an, the closer I was, they assumed, to embracing Islam.

It's a trip to hear Muslims talking about the magical power of the Qur'an. I have been repeatedly told by Muslims that Neil Armstrong, the first man to set foot on to the moon, had converted to Islam upon returning from outer space. While on the moon, Armstrong had heard the call to prayer and felt such heavenly emotions that when he returned to earth he straightaway converted to Islam.

My Muslim friends told me this so often and so emphatically that I finally did some research to find out if it was true. I found a whole Web site devoted to refuting that claim, with statements by Armstrong himself. It turns out that he did take a trip to the Middle East after returning back from space. He was asked by an Arab reporter what he thought of the call to prayer. His response was, "It is spacey." From there the rumor spread that Armstrong had heard the call to prayer in space and thus converted. His conversion was printed as fact in the major newspapers of several Islamic countries, including the one I was in. This rumor was able to gain legitimacy because Muslims really do believe the words of the Arabic Qur'an have a magical quality.

The Qur'an is the most treasured possession of the Muslim, and the reverence in which they hold it can hardly be overstated. Attempts to validate the Islamic faith almost always, in some way, return to the "miracle of the Qur'an." It is, in their opinion, their best weapon.

## The Benefits of the Ummah

Second, my Muslim friends attempted to woo me into Islam by showing me the benefits and blessings of being a part of the Islamic *ummah* (social community). They took advantage of almost any situation to point out how incredible it was to be a part of such a caring, respectful fellowship. I was most always treated with grace and hospitality. I was frequently invited over for dinner, and was given the place of prominence at most parties. These were the benefits of Islam, I was told, all available to me at the price of conversion!

Moreover, I was told that if I would just convert I could have up to four of their women to be my wives. And that, I was told, was just the beginning. At least 70 eternal virgins awaited me in heaven.

Muslims believe that the beauty, happiness, and solidarity of their communities is a primary benefit of Islam.

## Miraculous Proofs of Islam

Third, Muslims would often present me with folk tales about miraculous displays of power in the Islamic community as a way to prove to me that Islam was from God. Muslims are a very superstitious people, with a robust belief in the activity of angels, demons, and God himself. They pointed out that the marks on the palms of the human hands spell out the Arabic numeral for 99, the number of "Allah's beautiful names." I was shown rather dubious pictures of orange groves and arm-hair patterns that supposedly spelled out phrases from the Qur'an. Every village had a legend about an *imam* (Islamic religious leader) or other saintly figure who discoursed with angels.

---

Most Muslims live in a world where they see the supernatural as having an active presence.

---

Some Islamic clerics will maintain that such superstitious beliefs have no place in true Islam. Muhammad himself, as they point out, did not claim to have done any miracles. The only miracle of Islam, they'll say, is the Qur'an. But this has not stopped superstitious beliefs and practices from being rampant among ordinary Muslims. Whether orthodox or not, most Muslims live in a world where they see the supernatural as having an active presence.[1]

These are the three ways Muslims most often tried to convert me. What these do, however, is show you what is important to them about their religion. If you are going to share Christ with a Muslim effectively, you're going to have to pay attention to these three elements.

## Reasons Why Muslims Convert to Christianity

Now, let me reverse the question and show you why Muslims who convert to Christianity say they do so. I draw these reasons both from my own experience and from that of many lifelong missionaries. What's interesting is that you'll find that they mirror the three things above. They are exposure to the Bible, a supernatural intervention of some type, or an experience of the love in a Christian community.[2]

### Exposure to the Bible

Muslims most frequently cite exposure to a Bible as instrumental in their conversion. There is simply no substitute for getting the Muslim to read and study the Bible on his own, for at least two reasons.

***First reason: most Muslims are intrigued by the stories in the Bible.*** They are familiar with the names of many of the main characters, but the stories they have heard of them are incomplete. Where they may be closed to Christian doctrine, they are often open to the stories of the Bible.

Muslims, like Christians, believe that God has revealed his will primarily through prophets who spoke for him. Islam identifies 25 "major" prophets, beginning with Adam, Abel, and continuing on through Isa al-Masih (Jesus the Christ) and Muhammad, the seal of the prophets. Muslims believe the messages of these prophets to be found primarily in four holy books, the *Taurat* (Torah), the *Zabur* (writings of David), the *Injil* (Gospel), and the *Qur'an*.

The Qur'an and the Hadith (the collections of sayings and examples of Muhammad) do not contain the full accounts of the prophets, so the Qur'an instructs Muslims to consult the "people of the Book" for further information:

> If thou wert in doubt as to what We have revealed unto thee, then ask
> those who have been reading the Book from before thee (10:94).[3]

The Qur'an tells Muslims that Christians are their closest friends and that faithful followers of the Taurat (Torah) and Injil are of the one true religion:

Strongest among men in enmity to the Believers (Muslims) wilt thou find the Jews and pagans; and nearest among them in love to the believers wilt that find those who say, "We are Christians"; because amongst these are men devoted to learning, and men who have renounced the world, and they are not arrogant (5:85).

If only they (the people of the Book) had stood fast by the Law, the gospel and all the revelation that was sent to them from their Lord, they would have enjoyed happiness from every side. There is from among them a party on the right course; but many of them follow a course of evil (5:68-69).

Each prophet, Muslims believe, had a specific task on earth—something particular they were to add to the body of revelation. For example, Noah was the prophet who explained divine judgment. Moses was "the lawgiver"; Jesus was "the Word"; Muhammad is "the seal (the final conclusion)." Muhammad was to bring together all the strains of divine revelation into one perfect and complete sum, the Qur'an. Muslims are quite open to learning about the "special" contribution of each of the other prophets—a fact you can usually use greatly to your advantage. Let me illustrate.

### The story of Aisha

"Aisha" was an articulate and intelligent Muslim college student who lived next door to me in Southeast Asia. She loved to debate doctrine. One morning she approached me. I knew a debate was coming because she had that look in her eye. She asked, "Does the Bible teach you how to set up a fair and effective government?" I inquired as to why she was asking. She replied, "In our government class we have learned that the reason non-Islamic countries are in such disarray is because Islam is the only religion that prescribes how a government is to be set up."

I felt the hair on the back of my neck stand up. Christian political philosophy has always been an interest of mine. I was ready to explain how Christian political philosophy, as derived from the Bible, was superior to Islamic totalitarianism, and to refute her claims that Islamic countries are superior civilizations. But I did not. I simply told her that I was aware that the Qur'an did indeed give explicit instructions about how to set up a government and that, quantitatively speaking, the Qur'an and Hadith said more about politics than did the Bible (this much is true).

Knowing that she believed that each prophet had a special task from God, I told her that Jesus' special focus was the forgiveness of sins and eternal life. If a person is afraid to die, I told her, Prophet Jesus said he could help her. Of course, I knew these were deep issues that she, like all Muslims, wrestled with (as will be explained in the remainder of this book). I saw the fight leave her eyes. "Really?" she asked. "Prophet Jesus can help me with that?" "Yes," I said, "He has helped me. It's all in the Injil." "Do you have a copy of the Injil I could borrow?" she asked. "I think so," I said.

I watched through her window as she sat reading the New Testament I gave her for the rest of the afternoon. If you were scoring points in a debate, I probably would not have come out a clear winner here. However, on my scorecard of witnessing encounters, this one goes down as a "W."

**The second reason: God speaks most powerfully through His divine revelation.** As Martin Luther said, "The Bible when attacked should be treated like a lion in its cage. Rather than attempting to defend it, just unleash it!" Rather than defending the Bible or Christian doctrine, the Christian should unleash its power by exposing the Muslim to it.

This means that a *goal* in any witnessing encounter may simply be getting your acquaintance to read the Bible, rather than persuading them of the gospel. Let me share another story.

## The story of Solomon

My Middle-Eastern friend "Solomon" responded to a magazine ad for American pen pals. He was a young Islamic imam, and he intended through this opportunity to meet a Westerner he could convert to Islam. Ironically, the American with whom he was paired, "Danny," had the intent of using this correspondence to convert a Muslim to Christianity.

After two years of correspondence Danny offered to come and visit Solomon. The two spent a month together in Solomon's home in the Middle East. Almost every night, Solomon told me, until late into the evening, they vociferously argued doctrine. When it was time for Danny to return to the U.S., they had reached an impasse. Solomon defiantly thanked Danny for convincing him of nothing but to be a better Muslim. Danny asked Solomon to at least promise to read through the Gospel of John once. Solomon, because of his friendship to Danny, consented.

Solomon said that as he read the gospel the words pierced his heart in a way nothing ever had—not the Qur'an, or even Danny's arguments. Solomon read and re-read the Gospel of John, and within a relatively short time he embraced Jesus as the Messiah. Solomon's love for Jesus would eventually cost him his family and home. His family has formally disowned him, and he is currently exiled from his country. What inspired such commitment to Jesus was Solomon's exposure to the Word of God.

It is the Word of God that creates life. In Genesis 11, God's Word brought life in a "formless and empty" world. In John 11, God's Word brings a new birth into a new creation. That is why simply getting Muslims to read God's Word is the most powerful tool in bringing them to Christ. The Word of God is the channel through which the life-giving power of Jesus flows.

Therefore, my suggestion is that you use all possible means to get the Muslim to read the Bible! Use the passages from the Qur'an cited above to invite the Muslim to study the Bible with you. Say, "Hey, if you'd like to learn more about the prophets the Qur'an mentions, why don't we study them together in the Bible?" Become a master at retelling the stories of the prophets in a way that points the hearers to Christ.

## Miraculous Interventions

Missionaries of many different denominations have testified to miracles and supernatural visions among Muslims. Having been confronted so clearly with their evidence, even the most skeptical (such as me) have had to acknowledge the validity of such things. But you can't really build a strategy on "miraculous intervention." You can't program miracles—that's why they are called "miracles." But there are two things you can do to open the way for them and take advantage of them when they happen.

***Be prepared to acknowledge the validity of miracles or dreams.*** About half of all the Muslim conversions I have personally seen involved some type of dream. Let me share two personal experiences.

## The story of Mahmud

"Mahmud" was a 32-year-old Muslim who came to me with questions about the Injil (gospel). We had never met; he had only heard from a friend that I was an expert on the Injil. We found a quiet place and he began to tell me his story. A month prior, he said, he had had a dream. In this dream he walked alone in a gigantic, empty field. This field, he told me, seemed to him to symbolize his life. He felt alone, without purpose, true companionship, or direction.

As he walked through the field he heard a voice call his name from behind him. As he turned, he saw a man, in his words, "dressed in shining white clothing. I could not look on his face, because it was bright like the sun." This heavenly man reached into the sash of his robe and pulled out a copy of the Injil. "This," the man said to Mahmud, calling him by name, "will get you out of this field." Mahmud refused, as he knew it was "Christian literature." He told me he then woke up in a cold sweat, heart beating quickly, and feeling very afraid. He said he felt as if he had rejected a prophet. But he knew the price he would have to pay for following the Injil, so he brushed off the experience as only a dream.

When he fell asleep the second night, he found himself again in the same field. The "man" appeared again, again offering Mahmud the Injil. Again Mahmud fearfully refused. The third night when Mahmud went to sleep the man was there waiting for him. "This, and only this," he said to Mahmud, "will get you out of this field." Mahmud told me that, with trembling hand, he took it from the man.

Mahmud then turned to me and said, "My friend tells me that you are an expert on the Injil. Can you interpret my dream?"

(Here we go again...)

For the next two hours I explained the gospel to him. Though he still had questions, he didn't really doubt the answers I was giving him...after all, he'd been instructed by a divine messenger to listen. When I explained to him how Jesus had taken his sin on the cross, he said, with tears streaming down his face, "Allah...the Creator God, dying in my place? How could it be true? Oh, Allahu Akbar, Allahu Akbar [God is the greatest]!"

When I had seen that he believed, I asked him if he would like to be baptized. He said yes, and I asked him if he knew what such commitment might cost him. He paused, and said, "Yes. This is why it took me over a month to find the courage to come talk with you...But I concluded that the 'Man' in that dream must be Jesus Christ. And if he was searching for me, and wanted me to follow him, then it would not matter what anyone else could do to me. I would go with Jesus anywhere, as long as he goes with me."

Dreams of this nature make evangelism much easier! These dreams usually did more persuading in one night than I did in months of argumentation. Perhaps you grew up in a Christian tradition (like I did) that didn't really talk about them, and maybe you are skeptical of whether or not they could actually happen...Well, first, don't tell Paul, because he based his whole ministry on an appearance he received of Jesus! Second, you should realize that reports of miraculous dreams among Muslims are just too numerous and too consistent to be ignored.

However, while I think you should acknowledge the validity of dreams and visions, and even pray that God gives them, I don't think you should depend on them as your primary tool in making Christ real to the Muslim. God has commanded us to persuade others using the power of his word and our changed lives.

This is how the apostles worked. Luke says in Acts that "signs and wonders *followed*" the preaching of the gospel. It was Peter's explanation of the gospel (Acts 2:14-41) and the incredible love and generosity of the early church (Acts 2:42-45) that caused "great fear and awe" to come upon the watching community, caused them to have "favor with all the people," and caused God to daily "add to their number those who were being saved." Miraculous signs, if they come, should "follow" our explanation of and living demonstration of the gospel—never replace those things.

The greatest and most convincing act of power was Jesus' resurrection of the dead, proof for which is amply laid out in the Bible! Don't let your hope for a miraculous sign hinder you from using the *primary* means I just mentioned that God gave us to open blind eyes: the explanation of—and living demonstration of—the gospel!

Since the Spirit must enable a person to understand and perceive the truth of the gospel before they can believe (1 Corinthians 2:14-16; 12:3), whenever you present the gospel you are depending on a divine intervention *no less miraculous than a dream*. Blindness of the soul is no less hopeless a condition than blindness of the eyes. Thus, we must not only allow for divine intervention in the lives of our Muslim friend, we must depend on it!

***Make prayer the foundation of your ministry to Muslims.*** Since it is power from God alone that enables Muslims to believe, prayer is our most effective weapon. There have been times when I felt like there was nothing else I could do for my Muslim friends, and so I just prayed. Not just *for* my Muslim friends, but *with* them. I offered to pray for any of their families who were sick or had a need. God healed some of the people I prayed for. People around my village began to seek me out, asking me to pray for their sick relatives. I'll never forget the day that a group of children showed up at my door and asked if I would come to pray for one of their mothers. I heard one little boy explain to another one, "You must have this man come and pray for your mother. God listens to him."

God, you see, has always set his people apart from others by answering their prayers. Moses told the children of Israel that it was answered prayer, not brilliant knowledge or superior might, that would prove to the surrounding nations that they were truly God's people: "What great nation is there that has God so near to it, as the LORD our God is to us, for whatever reason we may call upon Him?" (Deuteronomy 4:7). When Elijah sought to demonstrate that his God was the only true God, he offered the "proof" of answered prayer: "You call on the name of your gods, and I will call on the name of the LORD; and the God who answers…He is God" (1 Kings 18:24). When Solomon dedicated the temple in 2 Chronicles, he asked that it be a place where non-Jews could come and have their prayers answered:

> As for the foreigner who does not belong to your people Israel but has come from a distant land because of your great name and your mighty hand and your outstretched arm—when he comes and prays toward this temple, then hear (him) from heaven…and do whatever the foreigner asks of you, so that all the peoples of the earth may know your name and fear you, as do your own people Israel (2 Chronicles 6:32-33 NIV).

In other words, miraculously answered prayer has always been a sign to non-Christians of the truth of the gospel. God's purpose is to show that he alone is powerful above all other gods (Psalm 96:4-5)! He wants us to pray, as Elijah, and Daniel, and David, and Solomon, and Paul, that God would make himself known. Jesus is the New Temple, and by praying in his name Muslims can "know God's name and fear him."

It is also worth mentioning here that Muslims are intrigued by the closeness to God Christians express as they pray (the reasons for which we will discuss in depth in chapter 5). Thus, praying *for* them and *with* them and *in front of them* is powerful. The Christian's intimate worship of God can have a powerful effect on the Muslim heart.

### The Love in God's Community

Many Muslim converts point to the love they saw in Christian communities as the reason they came to Christ. Community identification is central to salvation in Islam (this will be demonstrated in chapter 3). Relationships in the Islamic *ummah* (community) are usually superficial.

For many Islamic communities, what binds them together is a common enemy, not love. A proverb about the *ummah* where I lived was, "I against my brother; my brother and I against my cousin; my cousin and I against our village; my village and I against our country; my country and I against the West."

---

Allowing Muslims to see Christian
community in action is so important.

---

The fabric of the community often is maintained by shaming those who threaten it. Those who bring shame upon the *ummah* are often ostracized or even killed. This creates a lot of artificial shows of morality. Many Muslims will never let others get close to them for fear of what others might do when the "real" them is discovered underneath.

True Christian community, by contrast, is built on grace, openness, authenticity, forgiveness, and acceptance. Most Muslims have never seen this, even in their own families. When they do see it, they are drawn to it, for it is an experience of Divinity. God is love, says the apostle John, and when one experiences true love he experiences God. Jesus said that *the world would know* that we were disciples of the true Son of God by our love for one another.[4]

This is why allowing Muslims to see Christian community in action is so important. Invite them into your home. If they won't come to your church, let them experience prayer and fellowship meetings. For example, college campus ministries in the U.S. trying to reach foreign Muslim students would get much further if they befriended Muslims and brought them into their communities than if they only scheduled debates with them. A recent survey showed, as I noted earlier, that the vast majority of foreign Muslim students who come to a college in the U.S. will spend their four years there and never once step foot inside an American's home!

Incidentally, if you are trying to share Christ with Muslims overseas, you'll want to look for ways to show them Christian community in action. If you have other Christian friends there, meet as a church and invite Muslims into it.

You may take the Muslim need for community into consideration even in how you begin to share Christ with them. Rather than meeting with a Muslim one-on-one, try reading the Bible together in a small group. If Muslims can come to Christ together, then they are not just *leaving* something (the ummah), they are *coming into* something (the church)! Because following Jesus often costs Muslims their families, giving them a community to come into can go a long way in alleviating fear. There's an old proverb among missionaries to Muslims: "It is easier to 'group Muslims and then win them' than it is to 'win them and then group them.'"

## A Yearning Generation

Let me make one final observation. For the first time in history, Muslims in just about every part of the world have been exposed to life outside of their communities. Many Muslim college students, through international study, television, or the Internet, have started to question their faith and the assumptions they have grown up with. Just like Western students, many yearn for something more. College is the time in which Islamic extremists are chosen and developed. The gospel is also a radical message, and many of those college-aged students are ready for just such a message. Jesus' radicalism is unlike any they have ever heard. His message was not "Serve God and kill," but "Love God and die."

Present this radical message to Muslim students in your community. Many of the brightest Muslim students—those destined to become leaders of great influence in their countries—are in schools in "Christian" countries, near to some of the most vibrant churches! Does your church see how strategic a ministry it might now have with some of Islam's most influential future leaders?

If you are living or serving overseas, look for Muslim students who are reaching for something beyond what they've found. Invite them to learn the radical ways of Christ.

As we've seen, the primary three reasons given for why Muslims become Christians correspond to how they try to convert others—by showing the beauty and power of God's words, by promoting the love in their communities, and by pointing to supernatural signs of authentication. Islam is a superficial counterfeit of the true gospel. It prompts questions it cannot answer, and points to a God it cannot know. The gospel is the power and life that Islam seeks. It is God's Word in the gospel alone that has power. It alone reveals the secrets of the heart. As Muslims feel their souls laid bare by the Word of God many will conclude "surely God is among you!" (see 1 Corinthians 14:25).

The grace at work among communities of believers will show Muslims a depth of love they have not known in the ummah. By this they will see, as Jesus said, that you are the disciples of the true and living God.

The God of the Bible is the true God of miracles. He has historically distinguished himself from false, rival gods by displays of power. We can look to God to demonstrate, sometimes in miraculous ways, that Jesus is indeed alive. The resurrected, living Jesus shows that he can do what no other prophet could.

Drawing Muslims *toward* Jesus is our essential task, not drawing them *away from* Islam. Anthony Greenham, who recently published a study of the conversion patterns of Muslims in Palestine and Bangladesh, concludes,

> The converts [from Islam to Christianity] were drawn to [Jesus] through various means. These are God's miraculous involvement, the truth of his message, believers' roles, Bible reading and an array of other factors. Nevertheless, Jesus is always central. In contrast, very few were converted because they rejected Islam.[5]

How can we bring Jesus to them? By giving them his Word, demonstrating before them the radical love of the gospel, and by praying for God's miraculous intervention.

3

# Understanding What Your Muslim Friend Believes

One of things that makes Islam so attractive is its simplicity. Ask any Muslim, from the village peasant to the learned Islamic scholar, and they will tell you that Islam is built upon five pillars with five core beliefs. Islam's simplicity is proof to them that it is from God.

Understanding the five pillars and the five core beliefs and the role they play in the Muslim's spiritual life is essential for knowing how to engage the Muslim with the gospel.

## The Five Core Beliefs of Islam

The five beliefs are the core elements of any Muslim theology. Muslims of all nationalities, in all times, and from all traditions have held these five beliefs in basically the same form for over 1300 years.

### Allah

*Allah* is an Arabic term meaning, literally, "the deity." Muhammad's central message to the rampantly polytheistic Arab culture of his time was that there was one God, not many. He was the God who had revealed himself through Adam, Abraham, and the prophets. The primary sin in Islam is *shirk,* which means to worship other gods besides or in addition to God, blaspheme God, or "assign partners to God." Christians commit *shirk* when they worship Jesus as God, when they pray to Jesus or in Jesus' name, or when they refer to Jesus as the Son of God.

## The Prophets

Muslims believe that God's word has been revealed by more than 124,000 prophets (Arabic *nabi*—prophet, or *rasul*—apostle) through history. Muslims identify 25 primary prophets, however, 22 of which are mentioned in the Bible. Adam is number 1; Isa al-Masih ("Jesus the Christ") is 24. Muhammad, the seal of the prophets, is 25.

The prophets preached one consistent message from Adam to Muhammad: repent and return to God (see Qur'an 2:132,136). One thing to note is that each added something new to the body of revelation. Muhammad, in the Qur'an, completed the revelation and established it in its pure and final form.

## Angels and Demons

Muslims believe in an active spirit world. Many Muslims believe that two angels "sit" on their shoulders, one recording their good deeds and the other their bad. During prayer they will turn and address these two angels. When a Muslim dies, before he is taken to heaven, the angel that recorded his bad deeds is allowed to beat him in repayment for his bad deeds.

The *jinn*, or demons, are responsible for much of the destructive activity on earth. Muslims engage in a whole array of rituals, ranging from their sleeping habits to the wearing of amulets, designed to avoid the curses of demons and invite the blessing of angels.

## The Holy Books

Muslims believe that the messages of the prophets are found primarily in four holy books, the *Taurat* (Torah), the *Zabur* (writings of David), the *Injil* (gospel), and the *Qur'an*. Each book, when given, was an accurate and authoritative word from God. However, the Taurat, Zabur, and Injil have been corrupted by the Jews and Christians. The Qur'an was given to restore the message. Unlike the other holy books, however, the Qur'an cannot be corrupted and its message cannot be lost. Allah's supernatural protection is upon it, and it exists now on earth, in perfect form down to the smallest syllable, as it exists in heaven.

The Qur'an cannot be translated out of Arabic and still be considered, technically speaking, the Word of God. Muslims believe the actual content of the Qur'an is eternal and has always existed in Arabic. This is why they quote and pray the Qur'an in Arabic, even if they do not understand the words they are quoting. The words of the Qur'an have their power when they are spoken or written in Arabic, whether the hearer understands them or not. My Muslim friends were always trying to get me to listen to the "beautiful words of the Qur'an." I later learned this was because they thought it had the power to convert me. I sat through what felt like never-ending and excruciating recitations of the Qur'an in my living room. Reading the Qur'an well is considered an art. People who do it well are known for it and are given almost celebrity status.

---

If you pick up the Qur'an and start to read it like any other book you are likely to quickly become confused.

---

If you pick up the Qur'an and start to read it like any other book you are likely to quickly become confused. It is a collection of recitations given to Muhammad by the angel *Jibril* ("Gabriel"), arranged in no narrative order. The 114 suras of the Qur'an proceed from the longest to the shortest (with the exception of the first, brief introductory sura).

Some suras contain allusions to the stories of the prophets. Some contain prohibitions, condemnations, or instructions from Allah. Some extol the virtues of Allah. When the Qur'an does make allusions to the stories of the prophets, it often assumes the reader is already familiar with these stories and gives very few details to go on.

***The Qur'an's development.*** One of the things you will also likely notice is that the Qur'an appears to contradict itself (at least in tone) in a number of places. For example, in some places the Qur'an speaks of Christians and Jews as "people of the book" and as Muslims' "nearest friends":

> Nearest among them in love to the Believers (Muslims) wilt thou
> find those who say 'We are Christians,' because amongst these are
> men devoted to learning and men who have renounced the world,
> and they are not arrogant (Sura 5:85).

The Qur'an even tells Muslims that if they doubt the message that Muhammad is giving to them to check with the Christians, "those who have been reading the Book from before yours" (10:94). In other places, however, it commands the Muslim to slay the unbelievers (including Christians and Jews) and accuses them of heinous blasphemy. The reason for the difference is that Muhammad's understanding of his mission changed over the course of his life.

Muhammad first saw himself as the reformer of a wayward Christian community. He had observed firsthand the moral and theological corruption of the Christians he traded with. He believed that Christians had departed from the message of the Holy Books and that he was being sent as a prophet to call the people of God back to the truth, just like the prophets of old. He expected that while he might be resisted at first, in time the Christian community would come around, repent of its sins, and receive him as a prophet. Those suras that were written early in his ministry were laced with that expectation. He saw himself as their prophetic reformer. (Most scholars believe that Muhammad was illiterate, so he knew only what others had told him the Bible had said. He was sure that what he was hearing was corrupted and when he spoke the truth the Bible would back him up.)

As Muhammad's ministry progressed, however, he came to realize that Christians, on the whole, were not receiving his teaching. So he quit seeing himself so much as the prophet calling Christians back to the true way and more as the divine enemy of a hopeless corrupted Christian community that must be brought into submission. Those suras written later in his ministry are saturated with the tone of conqueror, not reformer.

Even Muslim scholars will tell you that understanding the historical context of the chapters of the Qur'an is essential to interpreting it correctly, though they will likely disagree with your explanation of why certain events happened as they did and what the significance of those events is for Islam.

*The Qur'an's authority.* Muslims believe the Qur'an to be the words of Allah, not the words of Muhammad. The book opens with the command, given to Muhammad by Jibril, "Recite." Muhammad, illiterate as he was, was given the capacity to recite the words Jibril gave to him, verbatim.

It is particularly interesting that Muhammad at first thought it was a demon, not an angel, who was appearing to him with the message (a fact Muslims will readily tell you). He went home to his wife (Bukhari 9.111), scared and convinced demons were possessing him. It was his wife, Khadijah, 15 years his senior, who convinced him that the angel was not a demon but the actual messenger of Allah.

The Qur'an is the only authoritative, divinely inspired book that Muslims will recognize. They are intrigued by the Old and New Testaments of the Bible and are curious about a lot of the information and stories within. However, they believe that the stories and teachings of the Bible are corrupted, so anything that contradicts what they believe is immediately rejected.

Practically speaking, they treat one other source as authoritative, the Hadith. The Hadith are the traditions, stories, and teachings others recorded from Muhammad's life. When detail about Muhammad's life is scant in the Qur'an, it can be filled in from the Hadith. The Hadith consists of three major traditions, those collected by Bukhari, Dawud, and Muslim. (You will see these names in references to the collections.) While the Hadith are not recognized to be the infallible words of God, they are an authority. What Muhammad did and said is regarded as the standard for how Muslims should live.

### The Final Judgment

Muslims' ideas about what happens at the final judgment would be one of the top two most politically incorrect beliefs (the other being their ideas about jihad—holy war). On the one hand, for those who have followed Islam faithfully, a luxurious paradise awaits. I was often told that three rivers flow through heaven: one of pure milk, one of pure water, and one of whiskey (a strictly forbidden substance on earth!). Believers can drink whiskey in heaven by the gallon and never become intoxicated. For faithful Muslim men, 70 "eternal virgins" await. (I never could get a straight answer on what "eternal virgin" meant.) I was even told that in heaven a man can marry multiple women, keep them in different quarters, and hide their existence from his other wives.

I also could not get a straight answer as to what faithful Muslim women had to look forward to in heaven. (The simple fact of the matter is that Muhammad did not talk—or apparently think—much about women and heaven. In one of the few places in the Hadith he addresses women and the afterlife, he says that vastly more women go to hell than men. See Bukhari 8.76.456 and also 2.24.541.)

More thoughtful Muslims will say, however, that these images are metaphorical. While heaven is indeed filled with unspeakable pleasures, the greatest pleasure, they say, is seeing Allah face-to-face.

On the other hand, for those who have lived wickedly, the torments of hell include "boiling water" and "pus." The Qur'an literally describes it as a "roasting place."

Muslims depict hell as a place where your specific sins are addressed (think Dante's *Inferno*, Muslim edition). Frequently I'd be waiting at a bus stop, and some guy would come through selling the most grotesque comic books showing sinners undergoing all kinds of torture...lead being poured into the ears of idolaters to boil their brains; the thief having his hand cut off, only to have it grow back and be cut off again over and over; the liar having his tongue cut out in the same manner. Believe me, you don't even want to know what happens to the adulterer.

Muslim beliefs vary on exactly who goes to hell and for how long. Most Muslims believe each person must walk a tightrope over hell into eternity, carrying their bad works on their backs. The more bad works you have done, the more likely you are to topple into hell. (More sophisticated Muslims will contend that this idea is also more a metaphor, but the concept is the same.)

The Muslims I lived with believed that almost everyone would spend a little time in hell, where his specific sins would be dealt with and purged through fire. The more sins you have, the longer you will be in hell. How long? No one knew. When I asked if there was anyone who would *never* get out of hell, they said that it was those who had committed the sin of *shirk*. I asked if that included me, and they said they didn't know (or maybe they did and they were just being polite).

## The Five Pillars of Islam

The five pillars of Islam are the five essential practices observed by faithful Muslims everywhere. As with the five beliefs, these practices are remarkably homogeneous in their expression, having been practiced in basically the same form by Muslims of all nationalities and all traditions for the past 1300 years.

### The Confession

The Islamic confession, known as the *shahada*, is simply, "There is no God but Allah, and Muhammad is the Apostle of Allah." This confession first acknowledges the absolute oneness of God (known as His *tawhid*). He has no rivals, no equal, no competitors, and no partners. This distinguishes Islam, Muslims believe, not only from polytheists, religious relativists, and atheists, but also from Christians, who worship Jesus, consider him equal to God, and pray in his name. Whenever a Christian ends a prayer "in Jesus' name," Muslims believe he violates the *tawhid* of Allah and commits *shirk*.

The confession secondly acknowledges Muhammad to be the ultimate arbiter of the will of Allah for mankind. Emir Caner and Ergun Caner, former Muslims, write,

> What seems like a simple statement is actually comprehensive in its scope. The admission of Muhammad as the final messenger of Allah places the believer within the prophet's belief system. There-fore, the Muslim maintains what the prophet believed, including that the Qur'an is the final and perfect revelation of Allah, that prophets are messengers to all people groups, and that angels do the will of Allah. In addition, theological tenets of resurrection, judgment day, heaven, and hell are accepted as factual.[1]

The *tawhid* of Allah is the core of Muhammad's message, and Muham-mad is the authoritative source on all things Allah. To become a Muslim, you must simply repeat this confession three times. That's it. Then you're in.

### The Prayers

The ritual prayers, known as the *salat*, are performed five times a day. Muslims face Mecca when they pray and should perform such prayers in a mosque when possible. They can be excused from the prayers in certain situations that make the prayer ritual impossible (such as during a woman's menstrual cycle, space travel, or rectal surgery). If missed, the prayers must be "made up" later.

The five daily prayers form the framework of every Muslim's day. My first day in an Islamic country, I was unexpectedly greeted by the 4:30 a.m. call to prayer being blared from the speaker next to my hotel window. I didn't know what was happening...I thought the city was being bombed. I got up in a panic, only to learn that this was what would greet me every morning I lived there. (Thankfully, over time, you get used to it and can even sleep through it.)

(For a while I couldn't figure out why so many of my neighbors were up walking the streets at 5:30 a.m. I'd look outside my window and it would look like "sidewalk rush hour." It was because they had all gotten up for prayer and had about three hours before work started so, with nothing bet-ter to do, they roamed the streets!)

The prayers are very important to the Muslim as a way of earning merit and removing sin. One of the Hadiths says,

> Narrated Abu Huraira: I heard Allah's Apostle saying, "If there was a river at the door of anyone of you and he took a bath in it five times a day would you notice any dirt on him?" They said, "Not a trace of dirt would be left." The prophet added, "that is the example of the five prayers with which Allah annuls evil deeds" (Bukhari 1.10.506).

A prayer said in the mosque is worth 25 times a prayer said at home or out in the market. The Hadith says that if a Muslim goes to the mosque with the sole intention of saying a prayer, every step he takes toward the mosque is translated into one additional reward in heaven and one sin taken off his account (Bukhari 1.11.620).

The essential part of the prayers is a recitation of Qur'anic verses, including the Islamic confession. A number of physical postures accompany the recitation of various verses. These postures are designed to signify some aspect of the Muslim's devotion to God. For example, the Muslim takes his hands and puts them behind his ears and then brings them down to his belly, showing he is hearing the word of Allah and bringing it into his heart. He bows with his head to the ground showing his absolute submission to Allah's will. After repeating the required recitations, he may offer personal requests to God.

---

If the Muslim comes into contact with any type of defilement (called *najis*) after they wash and before they pray...they must go and wash again.

---

An extensive washing process, known as *wudu*, precedes the prayers. *Wudu* is designed to cleanse the worshipper from all defilement. Muslims wash their hands up to their wrists three times; rinse out their mouths three times; cleanse the nostrils by sniffing water three times; wash the face from forehead to chin and from ear to ear; wash the forearms up to elbows three times; pass a wet hand over the whole of the head; and wash the feet up to the ankles three times, the right, then the left.

If the Muslim comes into contact with any type of defilement (called *najis*) after they wash and before they pray (which includes touching a non-Muslim, touching the genitals, using the bathroom, or even passing gas) they must go and wash again. I noted earlier that I lived with a Muslim family for quite some time. Their prayer room was down the hall from my quarters, and sometimes after the teenage children had done the extensive washing process I would hide in the shadows and then jump out before they got to the prayer room and touch their arms and hands and thus "defile" them so they had to go repeat the process. It was a real hoot, and I think deep down they enjoyed it. (For whatever it is worth, I would not suggest trying this at the beginning of your friendship with a Muslim.)

I seriously think that the closest a friend of mine and I ever came to bodily harm was when he accidentally defiled the Muslim *wudu* area. At a bus stop he decided he had to use the bathroom, and found a room with a little running water and what looked to him like a lavatory trough…and, well, you can figure out the unfortunate rest. Thankfully, a bus was leaving town the next moment, and we lived to see another day.

### Fasting During Ramadan

Ramadan is the name of the ninth month of the year on the Islamic calendar. That month is set aside for sunup-to-sundown fasting. (The Muslim year has only 354 days, and thus the month of Ramadan moves back approximately 11 days each year based on our calendar.)

During Ramadan, Muslims are not allowed to touch food or water from the first sliver of sunlight to when the sun sets in the evening. They take the fast very seriously—sincere Muslims will even try not to swallow their saliva during that time.

Of all the ways to violate Ramadan, having sex during fasting hours is by far the worst. If you have sex, even with your spouse, during fasting hours, you must fast for 60 consecutive days to make up for it or, if you are unable to do that, you must give 60 needy people the cost of one day's food.

All Muslims are expected to participate in the fast. The only exceptions are for those in extraordinary circumstances, for women ceremonially unclean, or for those in a strenuous job they can't get out of. Again, Muslims who miss a fasting day are expected to make it up. This does not mean, however, that a Muslim can just skip a day on a whim and plan to make it up later. The Hadith says,

> Abu Hurairah reports the messenger of Allah said: "Whoever breaks
> one day's fast of Ramadan without an authorized permission from
> Allah, he will never be able to redeem it (with another) day's fast,
> even if he fasts to eternity" (Dawud 13.2390).

The month of Ramadan is in some ways the most difficult and, in others, the most enjoyable month of the year. Reasons for difficulty are obvious, especially if you live in a desert or tropical climate. Where I lived, people usually worked during Ramadan for only a couple of hours in the morning and then went home to sleep. Afternoons during Ramadan were like living in a ghost town, except for the few souls who stayed awake and were in extraordinarily bad moods.

Ramadan is an enjoyable month, however, because of the evening parties that are put on. When the sun sets, food spreads like you would not believe are prepared for the faithful to feast upon. Where I lived, it was reported that food consumption during the month of Ramadan goes up, not down.

For me, it was a fun month. I got up early with my Muslim friends to eat a huge breakfast, worked for a few hours, napped in the afternoon, and then waited for sundown so we could party like it was 1591 (the year the Muslim calendar entered a new millennium). It was like being in college all over again.

In all seriousness, this month is extraordinarily significant to Muslims. It represents for them the greatest expression of their faith. Performing the fast is a great source of pride to them. It distinguishes them from the followers of other religions and proves, they believe, their moral superiority. Even those who are not faithful, practicing Muslims usually observe the fast! The societal pressures to conform alone are enough to ensure that. If you are living in an Islamic area you will be expected to respect the fast, at least publicly, and refrain from eating and drinking in their presence.

## The Giving of Alms

Muslims are expected to give 2.5 percent of their overall estate (in Arabic, *zakat*) each year to the poor. In some countries this is collected by the government, in others it is the expected freewill offering.

The Qur'an places the giving of alms as central to a Muslim's salvation (the Arabic term for almsgiving literally means "purification"):

- "Those who believe, and do deeds of righteousness, and establish regular prayers and give zakat, will have their reward; on them shall be no fear nor shall they grieve" (Qur'an 2:277).

- "Save yourself from hellfire even by giving half a date-fruit in charity" (Qur'an 2:498; Bukhari 2.24.498).

- "The Prophet said, 'Do not with-hold your money by counting it (that is, hoarding it), (for if you did so), Allah would also withhold His blessings from you'" (Qur'an 2:514; also Bukhari 2.24.513).

## The Pilgrimage to Mecca

Every Muslim is expected, if able, to take a pilgrimage to Mecca (known as the *hajj*) at least once in his life. This is usually the highlight of a Muslim's life. Those who have made the journey are given a special level of respect and even a new title (*hajji*). In that most Muslim countries are poverty-stricken, many Muslims will save all of their lives to have this experience.

A trip to Mecca accords the same merit to the Muslim as 50,000 prayers in a mosque. While there, Muslims go through a series of stations where they commemorate the Muslim faith. They make the journey from Medina to Mecca, visiting spots along the way. They symbolically throw stones at Satan at the site of three stone pillars (*jamras,* Bukhari 2.26.736).

The climax of the trip is circling and touching, if possible, the great black rock (known as the Kaaba) which was given from heaven to Muslims as a holy and sacred place. I watched this moment in the hajj on CNN and asked some of my Muslim friends what the significance of the ritual was. One of them told me, "Those that are there in Mecca are the most holy Muslims in the world. During that moment they are all asking Allah for the forgiveness of sins. Certainly out of all those Muslims there is one worthy enough that Allah can hear their prayer for forgiveness, and on that one's behalf Allah forgives the sins of all who are present." (Though one Muslim tradition says there is no such significance. Umar says in Bukhari 1.8.390-391 that Muslims touch the rock only because someone saw Muhammad do it.)

For many Muslims the *hajj* is an overwhelming spiritual experience. One friend told me what most stood out to him was the diversity of nationalities on the *hajj*. It was there he realized that Islam must be true, because it is so universal. Muslims everywhere, he said, of all nationalities and classes, are equal at the *hajj*, and this is surely a picture of how Allah sees the peoples of the world.

Many Muslims, however, come back from the hajj disillusioned. They did not "feel" what they were expecting to feel. They see Mecca—which is supposed to be the most holy city on earth—laced with injustice, unkindness, and crime.

Christian witness to Muslims begins with accurately understanding what a Muslim believes. Keep in mind there is often a difference between what orthodox Islam teaches and what the "Muslim on the street" believes—or between what "most Muslims believe" and what *your* Muslim friend believes.

For this reason, take time to listen to your Muslim friend. Ask questions. Try to understand and fairly represent what they really believe and not caricature or belittle them. Honor them by really taking time to understand them. Listening to them is an important part of teaching them.

The five pillars and five beliefs are simple and straightforward, but they represent a stringent captivity that Muslims live under. Performing the pillars is how a Muslim earns the favor of God, and Muslims live in fear of never having done enough. Later, specifically in chapters 6 and 7, I'll show you how the gospel of Jesus addresses these pillars, in some ways fulfilling them and in others overturning them.

4

# Misconceptions

When the average Westerner hears "Muslim," a number of images come to their minds—mostly negative. The same is true when a Muslim hears "Christian." Imagine the most biased anti-Muslim political pundit in the Western world describing Islam...that is the type of rhetoric Muslims almost everywhere are continually exposed to about Christians.

Thus, from the outset relationships between Muslims and Christians are challenged by suspicions they have of each other. This creates a lot of static in the lines of communication, which hinders friendship and genuine dialogue about important things. These are things you need to know about, understand, and overcome if you want to have a meaningful relationship with a Muslim.

Some of the things Muslims and Christians find most offensive about each other are indeed true, and disagreement about them simply cannot be avoided. However, *knowing* that these obstacles exist will help you deal with them prudently. Other things, however, that Muslims and Christians assume about each other are not true, and knowing how to debunk these myths will be essential in establishing a trusting relationship.

Let's start with what Muslims assume about Christianity. I'll try to show you where each misconception comes from, and how you can overcome it. Then we'll look at the misconceptions Christians often have about Muslims.

## Misconceptions Muslims Have About Christians

*"Christians worship three Gods"*

This one took me by surprise. I knew that the doctrine of the Trinity would be difficult for Muslims to understand (indeed, it is difficult even for Christians!). But I never realized how badly Muslims misunderstood it and how offensive what they assumed I believed was to them.

Several Muslims asked me how I could believe that God could have had sex with the Virgin Mary to conceive Jesus Christ. Christians are blasphemers, I was told, because they worship three Gods: God the Father, God the Son, and God the Mother. I asked my friends where they had heard that. From their imam, they told me. I asked their imam and he pointed me to the Qur'an, which recounts how Jesus was questioned by Allah as to whether he taught his disciples to worship himself and his mother as the Christians do (5:116). Later, in the same sura, Allah explicitly condemns the Christian doctrine of the Trinity.

Of course, orthodox Christians find this depiction of the Trinity equally offensive, and this is a good place to start. Monotheism was a core, defining tenet of Judaism, and Jesus and the apostles demonstrated no desire to undermine that tenet. Christians in no way worship "three Gods." While the nature of the Godhead is indeed a mystery, Christians can wholeheartedly agree with Muslims that there is only one God worthy of worship. Any discussion of the Trinity that undermines that foundational tenet is a serious error. (I will deal more with how to talk about the Trinity to Muslims in chapter 8. But for now, note that many of the analogies that Christians use to explain the Trinity are unhelpful for the Muslim, as they imply that there are three Gods or that God is simply one Person wearing three hats, both heresies denounced by the church.)

Christians agree that the idea that the birth of Jesus was the result of copulation between God and Mary is blasphemous. This is nowhere taught or implied in Jesus' birth narratives in the New Testament. Furthermore, Christian theologians have agreed for 2000 years that it is improper and demeaning to God to assign biological functions like eating, drinking, or sex to him. Like the Qur'an, the Bible teaches that God is a Spirit and does not have bodily urges and needs.

### "Westerners are all Christians"

MTV was big in the part of the world where I lived. Western music videos frequently featured rap stars or scantily clad women wearing Christian crosses. My Muslim friends assumed, naturally, that these performers were Christians and how they behaved is how Christians behave. I was once asked by a Muslim college student friend if I would throw her a "Christian" birthday party. When I asked what she meant, she said one with the drinking and smoking and dancing like she saw Christians doing on TV.

In addition, Muslims assume that America, Britain, Australia, Germany, France, and other Western nations are "Christian countries." Our presidents are assumed to be "Christian leaders." I was once asked, in fact, why "the church" bombed Iraq.

---

You must make clear that not all cultural "Christians"
are followers of Jesus, and Western nations
certainly do not represent "the church."

---

Most Muslims do not have categories, as Christians do, for those whose religion is only a cultural tradition and those who have actually made a choice to follow that religion. You are not "born again" to obedience to Muhammad, as Christians are to God; you are simply born in your family as a Muslim.

Most Muslims also do not make the distinctions, as most Westerners do, between "church and state." Islam is, by its very nature, a political entity, complete with its own social law codes. To be born in a Muslim community is to be a Muslim. "Islam" is often seen as synonymous with sociopolitical entities.

You must make clear that not all cultural "Christians," however, are followers of Jesus, and Western nations certainly do not represent "the church." You have to explain that Western governments and societies are not ordered as Muslim societies are. You may find it helpful to not even use the word "Christian" to describe yourself because of all the baggage that comes with the term. I often called myself simply a "sincere follower of Jesus Christ." In that way, I was inviting my Muslim friends to examine my life and behavior on my own terms, not on the terms of what they saw on television or read in the newspaper.

### "The Crusades never ended"

Because most Muslims see religions as political entities like their own religion, they see Western "wars" as extensions of the medieval Christian crusades to conquer Muslim lands. The conflict in Israel and the recent wars in Iraq, for example, are all Christian attempts to take Muslim land and institute Christian rule.

Whatever your views on the current political conflicts, you will most likely find it unhelpful to debate whether Western "Christianized" countries were justified in the conflicts. What we should make clear is that the church was not intended by Jesus to be a political institution that fought earthly wars. When Western countries act, they do not represent "the church." At those times in history where one institutional church did engage in war, it did so not because of what Jesus taught, but in spite of what he taught. Throughout his life, Jesus avoided any recourse of violence to establish his kingdom. His followers did the same.

Muslims are often unaware of their own violent histories, as they are given a very one-sided view of history. College-educated Muslims where I lived had *never heard* of the Jewish holocaust and were not aware of Palestine's role in the Middle East conflict. Most Muslims believe that Muhammad fought only defensive wars. They are often unaware of Muslim aggression in history or in current conflicts. They are also unaware of how the rest of the world perceives them.

If you choose to engage this topic, do so cautiously. Ask the Spirit of God to help you determine what will be helpful for them to know in bringing them to Christ, and only deal with that. We are not trying to win arguments, we are trying to win a person. All arguments must be submitted to that one end. God will, in the final day, set the record straight, establish justice, and vindicate all earthly wrongs. Our role is not to vindicate the righteous and restore justice to the earth, but to testify to the gospel of grace.

### "The Word of God has been changed"

Muslims believe that Christians have perverted the Words of Allah to support their beliefs. Some think that Christians have twisted the meanings of the words of Scripture. The Scriptures themselves are good; it is Christian misinterpretations that are the problem. Others believe the perversion is in the translation. The revelations in the original languages are good; it is the Christian translations that are in error.

You can, of course, show those who think we are twisting the meaning of the Scriptures what the Bible itself actually says. As I explained in chapter 1, the best thing you can do for a Muslim is get him to read the Bible. This is quite often sufficient, especially for the less-educated Muslims.

For those who think the errors are in the translation, you can show them the original languages. I found it helpful to have verses put up around my house in Greek and Hebrew, showing that I had a high regard for the original languages as well. (What if you don't know Greek or Hebrew? Not to worry—most Muslims don't know Arabic either. Simply showing them that you are aware of the original and that the translation you are reading is a faithful one will go a long way.)

More educated Muslims will likely claim that the error is in the actual Greek and Hebrew texts. The original revelation given through the prophet was good, but over time Christians rewrote the texts to justify their beliefs and behavior. This is an untenable claim on a number of fronts, one that even the Qur'an would disallow. We'll go into all that in chapter 9.

## Misconceptions Christians Have About Muslims

### "All Muslims are terrorists"

I said at the very beginning of this book that I was less concerned with Islam as a geopolitical movement and more concerned with Muslims as individuals. My goal is not to logically deconstruct Islam or to speculate about its political demise. I want to help you understand Muslims as *individuals*—how the Muslim you befriend is likely to think and act. In that regard, the political stereotypes most Westerners have of Muslims—that is, that they are violent jihadists plotting the death of the West—is likely not true of your Muslim friend, whether they live in Jacksonville or in Jakarta.

Much has been written about how Islam was established "by the sword," or how Muslims who engage in terrorist activity are simply obeying what the Qur'an tells them to do. It is certainly easy to find Muslims using the Qur'an to justify violence, and there is no denying that Muhammad was himself a warrior. Many Muslims will say, however, that violence now is called for only in the rarest of situations, should be handled according the strictest standards of justice, and should never target civilians. For example, Nadir Ahmed, a popular Muslim apologist who runs the Web site www.examinethetruth.com, said in a recent debate with former Muslim Ergun Caner,

> Islam does not demand the death of all infidels, but does pre-
> scribe violence against the infidels in certain circumstances, but
> at any time during the violence, the Muslim should work hard to
> try to broker a peace with the infidel, even if it will entail a great

sacrifice. But, at no time are innocent civilians to be targeted in that violence.[1]

Even when you give the Qur'an the most gracious benefit of the doubt, however, asking "What would Muhammad do?" will still lead you to a very different place than "What would Jesus do?" Violence in the name of God is an inextricable part of Islamic history and doctrine.

That said, most of the Muslims you encounter either in Western or in Islamic countries are not violent people. They are kind, peaceable people and they are embarrassed by the reputation of Muslims worldwide (though many are bitter about it, as they believe they have been depicted unfairly!). While there is a good chance they see world politics very differently from the average Westerner—that is, they may not see the 9/11 attacks as "unprovoked," or the wars in Afghanistan or Iraq as in any way necessary, or Israel as a victim in the ongoing Middle East conflicts—you will most likely find them warm, hospitable, and peace-loving.

I found my Muslim neighbors and friends to be some of the kindest people on earth. They let me live in their homes and become a part of their families. They were, for the most part, respectful of my culture and ideas. They were generous and caring. I daresay that, as a foreigner, I received a warmer reception than most foreigners do in my home city.

This is not to say that most Muslims don't believe Islam will one day rule the world and that they therefore tend to excuse violence done in the name of Islam. I simply mean that you don't usually need to fear that your Muslim friend is plotting your assassination. Some Christian apologists will insist that Muslims are peaceable *despite* Islam, and perhaps this is true, but they are peaceable nonetheless. Most are enamored of the freedom and equality in democratic societies. Most are very interested in Western culture. Most desire, but will never have, a Christian friend.

Arguing that Islam is inherently violent or that terrorists are simply following in the footsteps of Muhammad may be a good discussion to have in some formal debate contexts, but it will get you nowhere in most of the relationships you form with "normal" Muslims.

### "Muslim women all feel oppressed and unhappy"

Westerners often think of the Islamic woman as severely oppressed. She walks six feet behind her husband, staring dutifully downward, lives at the back of her house, never sees the light of day, can barely read or write, and is subject to her husband's sexual whims. We may think of Muslim women as unhappy, bitter, and longing to get out from under the oppressive rule of Islam and their dictatorial husbands.

This is often very far from the truth. Here are three things to keep in mind about the women of Islam.

### 1. The Qur'an and Hadith do indeed foster the oppression of women.

There is simply no way around the fact that the Qur'an and the Hadith are discriminatory against women. The Hadith says that 80 percent of the people who go to hell are women.[2] In explaining why the witness of a woman is equal to only half of that of a man in court, it reasons, "Because of the deficiency in their brains."[3] The Qur'an instructs Muslim men to warn their wives twice about misconduct, showing them the whips hanging on the walls before using them.[4]

Muslim men can marry up to four women, and can divorce any of them simply by saying, "I divorce you" three times. (I once asked if women could divorce men by saying, "I divorce you," three times as the men could. I was told this was not allowed for women because their emotions were too fickle.) The Qur'an says that Muslim wives "are like a field to be plowed."[5] Women are sexual objects, which is partially why they must remain hidden in the house and not interact with men. Muslim men often cannot conceive of relating to a woman any way other than sexually.

This does not even take into account localized practices such as female circumcision, religiously approved prostitution, or the double standards in punishing immorality. (Adulterating women are often put to death, girls who get pregnant out of wedlock are shunned from society—nothing equivalent is done to the man in most cases.) Islam was birthed in a society where women occupied a very low place, and Islam did very little to change that. Muslims will argue that Muhammad raised the status of women considerably. That may be true, but he certainly did not make them equal. For this reason, many missionaries have found that showing Islamic women their dignity in Christ is an immensely effective evangelism strategy.

### 2. Many Muslim men and women are in fact happily married.

No Muslim man I know personally has more than one wife. I heard of one man who did, and it was often brought up as a joke, like he was a weirdo or something. Many of the women and men I observed were, relatively speaking, happily married. They didn't "date" and "do romance" as Westerners are accustomed to, but neither were the women the demeaned sex-slaves Westerners often assume they are.

There were certainly exceptions. I had friends whose wives were rarely allowed out of the back of the house, much less out into the community. Furthermore, there are certain cultures in which Islamic women, on the whole, face great oppression and abuse. (For example, see Khaled Hosseini's excellent novel *A Thousand Splendid Suns*, which gives you a glimpse into the oppression of women under the Taliban regime in Afghanistan.) But by and large, women do not see themselves as oppressed.

**3. Women are often the most ardent defenders of Islam.** Despite Islam's history of oppression, women will often be Islam's most strident supporters. Many Westerners are shocked to find that they are often the ones most resistant to changing even ancient barbaric practices like female circumcision! Many Islamic women, especially in the Western world, call for reform in how women are treated in Islamic culture, but rarely for an end to Islam itself.

In other words, you are wrong if you think that Muslim women view themselves as victims in desperate need of your rescue, eager to convert out of Islam. As I said above, with patience and grace you can show women that God offers them so much more than they experience in Islam, and women often become the most fervent converts...but don't think it will be an automatic, easy sell.

I have included, in "Additional Resources" a list of great books on understanding and sharing Christ with Muslim women. If you would like to delve deeper, that is a good place to start.

### "Muslims worship a different God than Christians do"

Muslims claim to worship the God of Adam, Abraham, and Moses. Most missionaries find it therefore helpful to use the Arabic term for God, "Allah" (meaning literally, "the Deity"), to refer to God, and to explain that the God Muslims believe in, the God of the Prophets, was the God also present in bodily form in Jesus Christ and the One worshipped by Christians for the past two millennia.

You might ask, "But isn't the Islamic God so *different* from the Christian God that they cannot properly be called by the same name? Aren't we worshipping two different gods?" Believing wrong things about God and worshipping him incorrectly doesn't mean one is worshipping a *different* God. Many first-century Jewish people rejected the Trinitarian nature of God and that Christ was a messenger of God. Yet the apostles did not say that those Jews were worshipping a *different* God, just that they were worshipping the one true God incorrectly. Nor did the apostles come up with a new name for God to distinguish him from the Jewish God. Jesus did not tell the Samaritan woman he encountered at the well in John 4 that she worshipped the wrong God, but that she understood and worshipped God incorrectly.

---

When I would pray over a Muslim, asking for God
to heal in Jesus' name, I would often pray, "In the
name of Isa al-Masih, the One who is Lord."

---

Or consider the New Testament writers' use of the Greek word *theos* for God. *Theos* was, in its origin, a term for the capricious pagan deities of the Greek pantheon. A Greek *theos* was incredibly different from the God of the Old Testament. Yet, when Paul, John, and Matthew chose (under the inspiration of the Holy Spirit) a Greek word for God, they did not insist on the Hebrew *Elohim,* or even invent a new, distinctive Greek word for God, but instead used the pagan word *theos* and filled it with new, biblical meaning. As one longtime missionary friend told me, this should be a source of relief to English-speaking people. When the first missionaries to northern Europe chose a word for "God," they chose the Germanic word *got* which referred originally to Nordic deities such as Wotan, Thor, and Freya (whose names we still commemorate in the words *Wednesday, Thursday,* and *Friday*).

Muhammad preached many incorrect things about the one true God, but he made clear that he was referring to the God of the Old Testament, the God first revealed to Adam and Abraham. Thus, it is my opinion that it will be most helpful to start with the one, true revealed God of Abraham as the common ground to begin discussing the gospel with a Muslim.

That said, you might discover that with certain audiences, use of *Allah* or *Isa al-Masih* is more confusing than it is helpful. Which name to use is more of a practical question than a theological one. I once heard of a converted Muslim who said that he hoped one day he could be martyred as a testimony among his people for "Yesus Kristus" (a name and title deriving from the Latin form of Jesus' name). When asked why he did not use the Qur'anic term for Jesus, *Isa al-Masih*, he said, "I want it to be clear for whom I am dying: not Jesus the prophet, but Jesus the Son of God." Perhaps, however, there is a way to make that distinction without retreating to the Latin form of Jesus' name. When I would pray over a Muslim, asking for God to heal in Jesus' name, I would often pray, "In the name of *Isa al-Masih, the One who is Lord*," thus using a term familiar to them while filling it with biblical meaning.

When talking with Muslims about the gospel, we need to eliminate any unnecessary distractions. Misconceptions Muslims have about you can be unnecessary distractions and you should be aware of them and try to clear them up.

Another distraction comes when you don't really understand what a Muslim believes, so that they feel caricatured.

We live in a world of stereotypes. We can show a lot of love to someone simply by seeking to really understand them and by seeing them as they would like to be seen.

# The Muslim Salvation Code

If you're going to explain to a Muslim how Jesus can help him get to heaven, you must first understand what he believes will keep him from getting there! What I want you to see in this chapter is how drastically different the Muslim concept of "salvation" is from yours (a Western, Christian one).[1]

Many of the questions the gospel answers for us as Western Christians are ones that Muslims are not asking! But there are a number of questions about God and salvation that Muslims *are* asking, and I want to help you identify those. Then, in the next chapter, we'll see how the gospel answers their questions about God as sufficiently as it answers our own!

Okay...so let me summarize for you the Islamic understanding of "salvation."

## Islam Is Primarily Concerned with Offering Guidance, Not Salvation

Islam does not possess a corollary to the Christian doctrine of salvation. At first this might seem odd, since there are so many similarities between Islamic and Christian theology![2] But in Islam, people don't have anything to be "saved" from. They need to be forgiven of their sins...but this only comes by an act of God that he declares of his own choosing. Nothing we, or anyone else, can do can "guarantee" God's forgiveness. Nor does God *need* anything to forgive us (like Jesus' dying on a cross). He forgives whomever he wants, whenever he wants, by his own declaration.

Christians believe in *justification* and *atonement* for sin. A curse resulted from our sin—death; its debt must be paid if we are to live forever with God. In Islam, however, Allah simply speaks forgiveness. I was told that God wills forgiveness in exactly the same way he willed the first creation— he spoke and it was! One very sincere Muslim told me that he believed I was limiting God's power by saying that Jesus had to die on the cross for God to forgive us. Why, he asked, was God not able to just "speak" our forgiveness?

Islam also does not teach any corollary to the Christian idea of "original sin"—that is, the Christian doctrine that all men sinned in Adam and have been born with his fallen, sinful nature. Islam teaches that men sin because they freely choose it, not because they are born into it. Men are weak, but not depraved.

Muslims still believe that we can get to heaven only through Allah's grace, because we are all weak and we all fall into sin. But we don't, as Christians teach, need to be "born again." Since the old creation is not entirely sinful, we don't need to be made a "new creation."

This is really the heart of the difference between a Christian and Muslim understanding of salvation. As one Muslim theologian said, *"Every Muslim is his own redeemer*; he bears all possibilities of spiritual success and failure within his heart."[3]

The Christian Arabic term for salvation, *najat*, is found only once in the Qur'an (40:41), and there it means only an "escape from judgment."[4] In fact, when Islamic theologians talk about what Allah gives to us, they usually use the word *falah*, which means "success," rather than *khalas*, which means "deliverance," or *kada*, which means "redemption." Islam offers to men a "straight path" of guidance, which, if walked, can help them avoid judgment and prosper with God's blessing. Roland Muller describes Islamic salvation as

> the escape from the punishment of sin, not from the bondage of sin. It therefore does not involve a change of nature, but the bestowal of the privilege to enjoy sensual pleasures in Paradise...Salvation positively conceived refers to the enjoyment of physical effects in a pleasure-laden heaven.[5]

So, rather than "salvation," Islam offers "guidance" to mankind. Generally speaking, if you obey the guidance, your chances of being "forgiven" are increased (though not, of course, guaranteed).[6]

## Muslims Do Not Understand the Christian's Conception of "Divine Justice"

Muslims are bewildered as to why Christians insist that Jesus had to be crucified before God could forgive our sins. There are four reasons for this.[7]

First, to say that Allah's power to forgive requires a satisfaction of his justice would be, in their view, a limitation on his power. It implies to them that Allah *could not* grant someone entry into heaven, even if he wanted to, without this other thing happening first. His power to forgive, they believe, is like his power to create—he says only, "be," and it becomes. He says "forgive," and we are forgiven (Qur'an 16:40; 36:82). Jesus' death, they believe, is not necessary to "enable" God to forgive us. He does not require *anything* for *any* action he desires to take. As noted Islamic theology professor Suleyman Derin told me, "In Islam, there is never an '*A*' that must happen in order for God to do '*B*.' Allah simply says 'be' and it is."[8] So, again, just to be clear: Muslims view the Christian insistence that God requires an atonement for his wrath as a limitation on him, and thus an insult to his power. Or as another Muslim theologian said, "You are silly people in faith. Allah is not like a man. He can do what he wants. You have changed your religious books and your thinking is wrong."[9]

Second, saying that God required the death of Jesus to forgive us makes us more merciful than God, since we usually don't require "atonement" when we forgive someone we love. I was once told by a Muslim college student, "Our God is more merciful than yours! He doesn't require a bloody sacrifice to forgive us. In fact, *I myself* am more merciful than your God! If you asked me to forgive you on some matter, I wouldn't require you to *kill something* before I did! I'd just forgive you because we were friends. Why won't your God do the same?"

Third, Muslim theology insists that guilt is not something that can be "transferred" to another. The Qur'an is pretty definite on this one, "No bearer of burdens can bear the burden of another" (6:164), and "God does not hold any soul accountable except for its own deeds" (2:233).

Fourth, in Islam, sins are not so much "paid for" as they are weighed on a balance scale to determine if you have earned heaven.[10] If sins were paid for, it would be easier for the Muslim to think about someone paying in another's place. Since sins are weighed, however, the only consideration is what the individual has himself done. As one Muslim scholar remarks, there is no price paid once for all for sins that guarantees eternal life to all who trust in it.[11] Muslims see no purpose, then, for the cross, and believe the whole thing (even the event itself!) is a Christian fabrication (4:157).

Suleyman Derin, the Islamic professor I got to know, told me that Muslims deny *penal substitution* (the technical term Christian theologians use to refer to Jesus' removal of our guilt by paying our sin debt in our place). He declared,

> "Penal substitution," as Christians speak of it, is unjust and irrational. It punishes an innocent one in place of a guilty one, which does not bespeak justice. The Qur'an recognizes the injustice of this and denies it. Penal substitution is irrational, for it claims that God needs "this" in order to be able to forgive.[12]

*For these reasons Muslims often find a discussion explaining "why Jesus had to die" irrelevant.* (In other words, if you are explaining the "four spiritual laws" to them,[13] you are likely to become logjammed on the third law, trying to explain "that Jesus Christ paid the penalty for our sin, making it possible for God to forgive us." They question the logic of the premise on at least four counts!)

Now, don't go too far with this and conclude that Muslims don't understand the concept of "justice" at all...they do! The divine "scales" are a form of justice, one that Muslims believe angels monitor meticulously! The Qur'an says, "The balance that day will be true; those whose scale of good will be heavy, will prosper; those whose scale will be light, will find their souls in perdition."[14]

There are a number of things a Muslim can do to "tip the scales" in his favor. Performance of the five pillars is given great weight on the scales, but they vary in merit depending on when and where they are performed. As mentioned, a prayer said in the mosque is said (by many) to have 25 times the weight of a prayer at home; if said at the congregational gathering on Fridays, 500 times; at Medina or Jerusalem, 50,000 times; at the Kaaba in Mecca, 100,000 times.[15] Saying the *shahada* 200 times a day for a year is thought to erase 50 years of sins. The Qur'an says that performing *zakat* (acts of charity) can also take away sin (2:271). Many Muslims believe that a trip to Mecca absolves one totally from any sins committed up to that point. The omission of one of the pillars can sometimes be redeemed with a payment called a *fidya*.

However, in the final analysis, no act is sufficient to guarantee our forgiveness or necessary to secure it. God forgives, at will, for reasons we cannot anticipate or control! This is crucial to understand when you start talking with the Muslim about who Jesus is and what he did.

## Muslims Do Not See Salvation as Something Promised

Even the most devoted Muslims lack the "assurance" of God's favor and eternity in heaven. In addition to not knowing if they have done "enough" to weight the scales in their direction, Muslims believe God has a decree over their lives that they cannot change (*qadar*). That means that even the most sincere Muslims cannot guarantee that tomorrow they will even be in the faith, for Allah may have decreed that they will disbelieve. In other words, if Allah has decreed your damnation, all the merit of a lifetime will not help you! The Qur'an is disturbingly clear about this:

> Whom God doth guide, he is on the right path; Whom he rejects from His guidance, such is the person which shall perish (7:17).

> Those whom God, in His plan, willeth to guide, He opens their breast to Islam; Those whom He willeth to leave straying, He maketh their breast closed and constricted (6:125).

> But they are kept back from the Path. And those whom God leaves to stray, no one can guide (13:33).

> God has created you and your handiwork (37:96)!

> All things have we created under a fixed decree (54:49).

The impact of this belief is made painfully clear in a story I once read in the Hadith. Umar, a close, personal confidant of Muhammad and one of his most trusted generals, is reported to have said at his death,

> I am none other than as a drowning man who seeth possibility of escape with life, and hopeth for it, but feareth he may die and lose it, and so plungeth about with hands and feet…Had I the whole East and West, gladly would I give up all to be delivered from this awful terror that is hanging over me.[16]

Even Muhammad himself was unsure of his final destination! Muhammad once rebuked one of his companions for assuring the family of Uthman (one of his most trusted leaders) that Uthman had died in Allah's favor. Muhammad said, "Though I am an Apostle of Allah, yet I do not know what Allah will do to me!"[17] If Muhammad himself was unsure of his salvation, where does that leave the average Muslim?

Muslims *do* believe that Allah's mercy is abundant, just that it is never *promised*. Here's what you should learn from that: Your Muslim friend will probably not admire your bold proclamation that you are assured of eternal life.[18] They won't admire it because they won't understand it. They will most likely find it presumptuous, even blasphemous. I'm not saying you shouldn't say it. I'm just telling you how they are likely to react.

## Muslims Have Difficulty Believing that Jesus Was God Incarnate and Was Crucified

The two most essential things Christians believe about Jesus are that he is God and that he died for our sins on a cross. Muslims emphatically reject both of these.

The Qur'an expressly denies the central Christian doctrine, the Trinity. This, of course, means they also reject any claim that Jesus is God in the flesh. The Qur'an says, "They do blaspheme who say: God is one of three in a Trinity: for there is no god except One God...Christ the son of Mary was no more than an Apostle" (5:76-78). Muslims believe in *tawhid,* God's absolute unity and distinctiveness from his creation, which denies outright that there could be different "Persons" (Father, Son, and Holy Spirit) in the Godhead.

The Qur'an also directly denies that Jesus died for the sins of mankind. In addition to having problems with the whole logic behind Christ dying in our place, Muslims cannot conceive of any prophet of Allah dying in such shame and weakness, much less God himself! Seriously, God's got a reputation to maintain! Rather, as Muhammad triumphantly declares (4:157), Allah foiled the plot of those who wanted to kill Jesus, making them crucify another mistakenly in his stead. Allah had the last laugh, and it was the attempted killers of God's prophet who were humiliated. Allah is tricky like that.

The bottom line for Muslims is that God will not suffer and cannot die. That is *very* important to realize. It is because Muslims believe these two things that they deny the cross. When a Muslim argues against the historicity of the cross, it is not because he fails to see the historical evidence for it, but because he fails to see how it could have any purpose in God's plan. Our sins don't need to be paid for, and God won't be humiliated. Why then would God come and die on a cross?

## Muslims Feel Distant from God

The Bible teaches that because of mankind's fallen condition, all men "feel" separated from God, instinctively. As I touched on at the beginning of this book, the result of our sin, Genesis 3 says, was a feeling of nakedness and shame—the feeling that we are exposed, rejected, and guilty. Before the Fall we were naked but did not mind it because, as the early Church Fathers said, we felt "clothed in the robe of the love and acceptance of God."

Now, however, stripped of the clothing of God's acceptance, we feel "naked." And just like Adam and Eve we search, instinctively, for a covering. We want something to cover our sense of shame and rejection and hide us from the all-knowing eye of God. At the same time, we long to be reunited to God, to fill the gap left in our lives by God's departure.

What most people turn to for covering is religion. Doing certain things, they believe, will cover their nakedness and make them acceptable to God.

> Before the Fall we were naked but did not mind it because, as the early Church Fathers said, we felt "clothed in the robe of the love and acceptance of God."

This is what Muslims are doing with Islam. If they follow the tenets of Islam, they believe, they will be accepted and loved by Allah again! However, just as Adam and Eve found that their covering of leaves was insufficient to clothe them before God, Muslims (and people in all religions) sense that their religious covering has not taken away their shame and guilt either. So they live in perpetual fear that they have not done *enough*. They sense that something is still not right between them and God. They feel distant because they *are* distant.

### The Effect of Tawhid

Muslims have an additional problem when it comes to feeling close to God. The doctrine of *tawhid* teaches that God not only feels distant, he *is* distant. One Sunni imam told me that Allah is physically in heaven and he does not *in any way* "dwell" on earth. His throne, he said, is high above the earth—sitting on the top of the seven heavens! The lowest of the seven heavens is the stars that we see, and beyond the stars are six more layers separating us from God. Each layer is progressively larger than the former, with each comparing in size to the previous one like "the entire desert compared to a single ring which fits upon a man's hand."

Think about that for a minute…The expanse of the stars is like a ring in the desert compared to the size of the heaven that surrounds it, and again and again six more times! That's how far God is from us, according to Sunni Islam. The Sunni imam told me that this of course doesn't mean that God can't see and hear us, because Allah has perfect vision and hearing. But what this does do, however, is rule out any sense of intimate knowledge of God and *any* type of "fellowship" with him on earth (Qur'an 10:3; 2:255).[19]

Even the relationship Christians believe Adam and Eve had with God in the Garden is too intimate for Muslims. The only time the Qur'an says that God is close, it uses the analogy, "God is as close to you as the sword to your jugular vein"—not exactly a warm and fuzzy affirmation.

Not all Muslims hold such an extreme view of Allah's transcendence, but suffice it to say that most Muslims find the Christian description of God as "everpresent" and "in our hearts" confusing. To some, it may be intriguing, but to most others, blasphemous.[20] As Suleyman Derin, an Islamic professor friend, says, "The transcendence of Allah is the most essential difference between Islam and Christianity."[21]

Furthermore, the doctrine of *tawhid* prohibits using human relationships, such as "Father," "friend," or "son," to describe God's relationship to us. God is in no way, either by distance or by relationship, close to us.

The point of "salvation" in Islam is not to *know* God, but simply to *obey* him. Whereas Jesus said that his purpose was to help us *know* God (John 17:3; 1 John 5:13), the Qur'an is given so that man might walk obediently in "the Straight Way." Muslims are often shocked at how much "self-disclosure" there is of God in the Bible…how he walks with people, talks with them, seems to want to know them, and is intimate with them. *Islam* literally means "submission," and *Muslim* means "one who is submitted to Allah."[22]

### Attempting to Narrow the Gap

One thing that is interesting on this front is how folk Islam has attempted to fill the gaps left by orthodox Islam through a dizzyingly extensive system of superstitions. Technically, Muslims are resigned to the pre-ordained will of Allah. But practically, author Bill Musk says, they are rampant manipulators.[23] In just about every Muslim culture you'll find an elaborate network of traditions, superstitions, and mediums that demonstrate Muslims' obstinate refusal to submit to the "unchangeable" will of a distant God.

The most fascinating, and most common, of these is the worldwide Islamic phenomenon known as *Sufism*. Sufis attempt to interact with Allah's Spirit through meditation and ecstatic experiences.

Orthodox Islamic clerics first viewed Sufism, which was birthed almost 900 years ago, as a menace and tried to suppress it. They were unable, however, to resist its mass appeal. Eventually, in the twelfth century, the well-respected Islamic scholar al-Ghazali brought Sufism into the mainstream of Islam.[24] Though Sufism is still not technically "orthodox," it has a significant influence in almost every Islamic society.

To understand Sufism's influence on Islam, think of it like the influence of Pentecostalism in Protestant Christianity. Pentecostalism is not "officially accepted" in many mainline Christian traditions, but it has had considerable influence on Christian worship and thinking at almost every level. People in Baptist, Methodist, Presbyterian, and nondenominational churches worship and think and talk about God differently because of Pentecostalism's widespread persence.

In the same way, there are few Islamic communities that have not been affected by Sufism's call for intimacy with God. Phil Parshall estimates that 70 percent of all Muslims are acquainted with some Sufi order and millions are significantly shaped in some way, by the Sufi understanding of Allah. Sufism is now as much a description of contemporary Islam as it is the title of a sect.

Seeing how "irresistible" Sufism has been to Muslims worldwide shows you something about how they long for a closeness to God that Islam does not seem to be able to give to them.

## Muslims Feel the Need for Purification to Stand Before God

Almost all the Muslim prayer rituals concern the believer's need to purify oneself enough to stand before Allah. As I mentioned in chapter 3, there are a number of substances which are considered *najis* (filthy), and if a Muslim comes into contact with any of these she must cleanse herself thoroughly before seeking an audience with God. The list of these substances is numerous...including pus, blood, dogs, pigs, profuse sweat, sexual fluids, flatulence, menstrual cycles, and dung.

Cleansing from *najis* is called *wudu*. Any Islamic theology text will have a huge section on the *wudu*, and clarifications on the *wudu* abound in the Hadith.[25] Before prayer Muslim believers must vigorously wash the face up to the hairline, the earlobes, the hands up to the elbows, the inner parts of the nostrils, and the feet up to the ankles. The ablution is rendered invalid if the participant passes gas, faints, sleeps with his legs uncrossed (crossed legs guarantee that flatulence has not occurred!), experiences sexual arousal, touches his genitals, touches a member of the opposite sex, or comes into contact with any other *haram* (forbidden) substance before he prays. Touching a pig necessitates the Muslim wash the polluted area seven times with both sand and water.[26]

It is interesting to note here that Islamic theologians have given a deeper, spiritual meaning to the *wudu*. The Sufis talk about a "soul purification" that correlates to outward washing. They describe forgiveness as "soul cleansing" and the final state of the believer in Paradise as "souls shining from the final washings of *wudu*." *Sufi* literally means "purity." One reason Sufism is popular among Muslims worldwide is because it offers a way to stand clean before God! (This desire, however, is not limited to Sufism: A friend of mine who was a *very* strict Sunni Muslim teacher told me that heaven's greatest reward will be to stand face-to-face with Allah, in whose presence he will, at last, be perfectly clean.)

A huge problem for the Muslim, then is *how* to achieve an inner purification sufficient to stand in Allah's presence. Muslims believe that repentance and performance of the Islamic pillars are all that God demands we do in preparing ourselves to stand before him. Yet how is it consistent to say that purification from *najis* (physical impurities) requires a vigorous washing process in addition to repentance, *but purification from inner impurities requires only the repentance?*

After all, if all sin is impurity, then, the physical cleansing of the outer defilement should indicate a correlating process for inner defilement. If the physical defilement of dogs, swine, or excrement must be cleansed by sand and water, then for the Muslim to feel cleansed from such spiritual defilement as blasphemy, hypocrisy, or adultery, much more must be required! This is a question I began to ask a lot of my Muslim friends—and one that, as I will explain in the following chapter, really opened up a pathway for the gospel.

Muslims, you see, have a built-in desire to *feel* pure before Allah, which orthodox Islam *does not, and cannot, satisfy.*

## Muslims Live with a Sense of Shame

You won't live among Muslims for long before you'll notice how devastating it is for a Muslim to be shamed. A man who shames his hometown by acting immorally or disrespectfully will likely be driven out from his community. A Muslim girl who shames her family by getting pregnant out of wedlock will likely face exile, if not execution, to restore the family's honor. I once asked a close Muslim friend, "Why do I never see any unmarried pregnant girls in this town? Does that stuff just not happen here?" He laughed and said, "Oh yes, it happens. But once she does get pregnant, you are likely never to see her again."

Many Muslims live in fear of being exposed. Exposure of who they really are could lead to shame, rejection, or death.

## Muslims Seek an Intercessor

The vast majority of Muslims look to the intercession of Muhammad and other saints as an aid to their salvation. One popular Sunni theologian explains,

> We believe in the special great Intercession of the Prophet Muhammad, peace be upon him. He will plead with Allah, after His permission and on behalf of mankind...They will go to Adam, then Noah, then Abraham, then to Moses, then to Jesus and finally to Prophet Muhammad.[27]

Interestingly, orthodox Islam seems to forbid the use of an "intercessor" who can plead your case before God and increase His chances of blessing you or accepting you into heaven.[28]

However, the Qur'an itself affirms "intercession" in a number of places: "Who is there that can intercede in His presence except as He permitteth?" (2:255);[29] "Those around God's throne sing glory and praise to their Lord; believe in Him; and implore forgiveness for those who believe" (40:7); and "Those whom they invoke besides God have no power of intercession; only he who bears witness to the Truth" (43:86).

Whether it is orthodox or not, most Muslims seek the help of an intercessor. In chapter 3, I told of watching live segments from the *hajj* (pilgrimage to Mecca) on CNN with some Muslim friends. As the cameras showed all the Muslims circling the great Kaaba, I asked my friends what was happening. One explained, "They are all confessing their sins and begging Allah for forgiveness. We figure that those are a million of the best Muslims in the world, and out of that million, surely one is worthy enough to be heard, and on that one's behalf, Allah forgives the sins of all present! That's why each Muslim comes home from the *hajj* with a clean slate of sins." People are saved in the *hajj* by means of the intercession of a fellow Muslim.

Most Muslims look to Muhammad himself to intercede for them on judgment day. They hope that by closely following his example of living they can escape God's judgment. Many believe that by visiting his tomb they can gain *baraka* (Arabic for "blessing and help for salvation").

---

The notion of an intercessor is...
"a last hope for uneasy minds."

---

Sufi Muslims believe in a special type of intermediary called a *pir*, who is so saturated with God that his very breath contains the power of God. The *pir* transmits spiritual power to his disciples by touching them, teaching them, and breathing on them. The *pir* is a "little manifestation of God," who substitutes for "the ultimate *pir*, the Prophet Muhammad."[30]

Finally, as Bill Musk's two books, *Touching the Soul of Islam* and *The Unseen Face of Islam*, show, there are a staggering number of amulets, trinkets, and superstitions that Muslims in almost every culture use to ward off evil and increase their chances of heaven.

Muslims use these many forms of intercession to try to bridge the gap between them and Allah and to try to escape the hopelessness they feel under his *qadar* (decrees). The notion of an intercessor is, as Roland Muller says, "a last hope for uneasy minds." In fact, even if the Qur'an never encouraged intercession, Muslims would probably seek it anyway. Their troubled, fearful consciences desperately need it.

## Muslims Understand that Life Should Be God-centered

The Islamic creed insists that Allah is alone to be exalted in Muslims' lives and worship, and that he is to have no "partners." Muslims repeat this multiple times a day. Listen to a Muslim talk about God, and you will hear words like "only," "alone," "most," and "*all*" (as in all-powerful, all-forgiving, all-merciful, all-loving) sprinkled throughout.

However, Islam is, in very demonstrable ways, centered on man. (Islamic scholar Abdullah Yusuf Ali admits this in the foreword to his translation of the Qur'an: "The central subject of the Qur'an," he says, is "man, not God.") The Qur'an is a book about *what man must do* to obey God's will, not about how to know God, glorify him, and enjoy him. Think about it… Islam teaches man to look to *himself* for salvation.

Furthermore, Islam glorifies the man Muhammad—practically, at least, if not doctrinally. Every time a Muslim prays he mentions the name of Muhammad in the same sentence with the name of Allah! Muslims hope for help from the man Muhammad on Judgment Day. He is their hero. Watch the news, and you'll see that it's insulting *Muhammad* that elicits the strongest, most violent reactions from Muslims.

The takeaway here? Showing how it's the *gospel* that most exalts God will be a key in demonstrating its truthfulness. More on that in the next chapter.

Let me summarize: The most important things to remember about how Muslims understand salvation when sharing the gospel with them are

- Islam is primarily concerned with offering guidance, not salvation.

- Muslims do not understand the Christian's conception of "divine justice."

- Muslims do not see salvation as something promised.

- Muslims have difficulty believing that Jesus was incarnate God and was crucified.

- Muslims feel distant from God.

- Muslims feel the need for purification to stand before God.

- Muslims live with a sense of shame.

- Muslims seek an intercessor.

- Muslims understand that life should be God-centered.

Using these nine insights as a guideline, the next chapter will show how you can shape a gospel presentation that will be compelling—through the power of the Holy Spirit—to a Muslim.

6

# Re-coding the Gospel
## A "Gospel for Muslims"

In the last chapter we saw what questions Muslims are asking about salvation. Now I want to show you how to present the gospel in a way that connects with those questions.

When Western Christians present the gospel, the "problem" is usually guilt, and forgiveness (or, more technically, justification) is the answer. But, as I showed you in the last chapter, Muslims find the concept of "Christ paid our sin debt" difficult to grasp for a variety of reasons.

What Muslims are confronted by, however, on a *daily* basis (through their prayer and worship rituals), is that they are *separated* from God and are *defiled* before him. And just as the gospel provides forgiveness for the guilty soul, the gospel provides cleansing, restoration, and victory for the *defiled, shamed, alienated,* and *defeated* soul.

What we're after here is a "gospel for the Muslim." Now, to be clear, to say that there is a "gospel for the Westerner" and a "gospel for the Muslim" does *not* mean that there are two different gospels or that there is more than one way to be saved. Paul talked about Peter being commissioned with a "gospel for the circumcised (Jew)" while he was given a "gospel for the uncircumcised" (non-Jew, see Galatians 2:7). Yet both Peter and Paul preached salvation in Christ by grace through faith in his finished work, and both are clear that there is only one gospel by which man can be saved (see Peter's words in Acts 4:12 and Paul's in Galatians 1:8).

However, Peter, preaching to the Jews, emphasized different elements of the gospel than Paul did: Jesus as the fulfillment of prophecy, as the way to purity before God, as the promised One who restored the kingdom, and as the One who brought an end to the curses of the law (see Acts 2:14-41; 1 Peter 1–2).

Paul, on the other hand, preaching to non-Jews, tailored "his gospel" to their questions and experiences, which were different than those of most Jews. Paul emphasized the gospel as a fulfillment of mankind's longing for meaning, as God's righteous judgment on all ungodliness, and as the way of knowing the God of Creation (see Acts 17:22-31; Romans 1:18-32). It is the same gospel, but presented differently to address different questions.

The same will be true for the Muslim. There is one gospel by which both Westerner and Muslim must be saved, but it must at times be expressed differently so that each can more readily grasp it.

Much of what I'm going to share with you in this chapter comes from my own trial and error with Muslims (which isn't finished yet!), as well as some interaction with the early Church Fathers (Irenaeus, Athanasius, the Cappadocian fathers, and others). I did my doctoral work on the way the early church talked about salvation at Southeastern Baptist Theological Seminary. I found during that time that the Church Fathers seemed to have an incredible amount to say to Muslims—primarily, I believe, because they often approached salvation from a very similar vantage point as Muslims—that of being separated and defiled before God. As with Muslims, a salvation that could remove their defilement, conquer sin and death, take away their fear and shame, and restore them to God resonated with them. (This makes sense because, after all, Muslim culture has more similarities to the culture of the early church than it does to our modern Western culture!) So, I believe we'll find in the early church's ways of talking about salvation some really good help for presenting Christ to Muslims.

## A Gospel for the Westerner and a Gospel for the Muslim

Three key words define Western presentations of the gospel. The first is *formula*. Western presentations of the gospel are epitomized by Bill Bright's "Four Spiritual Laws," variations of which have been popular among Western Christians for years. In the "Four Spiritual Laws," we outline four propositions about God. These propositions, explained in order, like premises in a syllogism, compose a "formula" for salvation.

The second word is *forgiveness*. For Westerners, the primary problem we sense is judicial guilt before God, and so the need that must be addressed by salvation is forgiveness.

The third word is *death*. It was by his death that Jesus took care of our guilt. He purchased our forgiveness and removed our guilt.

This is, of course, an accurate (and essential) reading of the gospel. However, Muslims react against *all three elements* of this presentation. The very idea that God must behave according to "laws" is offensive. And so is the logic behind Christ needing to pay a sin-debt so God could forgive us, as Muslims reject that God requires something in order to be able to forgive (see chapter 5). Furthermore, Muslims have great difficulty seeing God as a victim who died in weakness.

Their "problem" with these things doesn't make any of them less true. After all, Paul said that the preaching of the gospel would be foolishness to those outside of Christ! It's just that Muslims are wired to react against them. (Though, I hasten to add, many Muslims have found Christ through such presentations.) But I want to suggest to you that, in light of the questions Muslims are already asking about salvation, our gospel presentation might be *more* effective if built around these words: *cleansing, victory,* and *story.* The Bible is the *story* of how Jesus Christ came to earth to *remove our defilement* and shame and *defeat* the curse of death.

---

It is because Jesus paid our sin debt that we can be cleansed and have fellowship with God again.

---

I'm not suggesting that you can ever make the cross "inoffensive" to a Muslim.[1] If you do, you're presenting the wrong cross! Christ's death on the cross will *always* be a scandal, Paul says, no matter how presented. However, presenting the dimensions of Christ's work that speak to the questions Muslims are already asking about God (such as those about cleansing and restoration) may help better connect the gospel to their lives. If we can show how Christ's substitutionary work removes their defilement, conquers God's enemies, and reunites them with God, they may not see it as an irrelevant proposition.

I also want to be careful to not imply that *cleansing* and *forgiveness* are two fundamentally different things. They are not. When 1 John 1:9 says that we are "cleansed" to have fellowship with the Father, it says this happens by the "faithful and just" forgiving of our unrighteousness. It is *because* Jesus paid our sin debt that we can be cleansed and have fellowship with God again. However, *emphasizing* the cleansing metaphor, and that through this cleansing we can stand in God's presence again, has more appeal to the Muslim than simply saying that Jesus settled our outstanding accounts at the register of God's justice.

So, let's examine those three things one at a time: *cleansing, victory,* and *story.* We'll look at each one and then see how it addresses the questions we looked at in the previous chapter.

## 1. Cleansing

### The Gospel Gives Purification from Sin

The gospel meets the Muslim's need for cleansing from defilement. Jesus explained that what defiles a man is not something he contacts in the outside world, but something that comes from within his heart (Matthew 15:18-20). The outward "defilement" with which Muslims are consumed is only a symbol of what truly defiles, sin in our hearts. As I pointed out in chapter 5, if the physical defilement of dogs, swine, or excrement must be cleansed by sand and water, then to be cleansed from spiritual defilement such as blasphemy, hypocrisy, or adultery, much more must be required!

The gospel teaches that the blood of Jesus is the only cleansing agent strong enough to remove the contaminants and corruption that separate men from God. The blood of the cross is *wudu* for the heart, able to cleanse it from *najis* (filth) and defilement. It releases the believer from the vestiges of his contact with the *haram* (that which is forbidden) and brings him face-to-face with God.

### The story of Diana

Once I asked an Islamic friend to explain to me why she washed as she did. She explained it was to remove all the *najis* with which she had come into contact throughout the day. I asked her what was the most "*najis*" thing of all. Her first answer was "pork." She explained that contact with pork required a vigorous, sevenfold scrubbing.

I then asked her if there was anything that might be filthier to God than pork. After a while, she said she supposed idolatry was the filthiest thing of all to God. I asked *where* idolatry took place. She said, "the heart." I asked, "So, you cleanse the body vigorously, but how do you cleanse your heart?" She said, "We just repent of our sin, and that cleanses us." I objected, "You can't just repent of touching the pork, you must also wash. How is repentance able to cleanse the heart of idolatry but not the hands of pork, seeing that idolatry is filthier than pork?"

She thought for a moment and then said, "That is a great question. I don't know." I continued, "Every time you talk to God you do so with a filthy heart. It's kind of like your *imam* came over to eat at your house. You had cleaned up everything in the house to honor his coming. But when it came time to serve dinner, you brought out the head of the pig. According to Jesus, this is what you are doing when you pray with a sin-tainted heart."

My friend seemed to understand. I explained to her that we Christians believe that the blood of Jesus is the cleansing for the soul. Later on, through this understanding and the continual love and prayer of her Christian friends, she put her faith in Christ.

Many of my Muslim friends were gripped by the story of Jesus' healing of the woman with a menstrual bleeding disease in Matthew 9:18-26. Muslims understand immediately the sense of rejection this woman lived with. (Muslim women are not allowed to participate in prayers or fasting while in their menstrual cycle.) To think of a woman who for years had been unable to serve or pray to God was deeply moving to them! They recognize that she lived with a sense of alienation and despair, wondering if she would ever be accepted by God and his people—a sense of alienation that most of them have experienced at some point in their own hearts. When they learn that this woman has the audacity to touch the "Holy Prophet" in her defiled condition, they visibly react—because usually, when a clean thing touches an unclean thing, the clean thing becomes unclean. But to their surprise, Jesus does not recoil in disgust. He calls her "daughter," and assures her that her sins have been forgiven. With Jesus, touching the unclean thing not only did not make him unclean, but made the unclean one clean!

What we are showing Muslims is that it is through the death of Christ that God restores the fellowship to the "unclean." Kenneth Cragg, a longtime missionary to Muslims, used to say, "The forgiveness of such as ourselves is not a wave of the hand, or the lifting of a finger, but the restoring of a fellowship."[2] The cross was the only way that God could look upon, and have fellowship with, the unclean. The blood of Jesus Christ cleanses us from all unrighteousness so we can have fellowship with God (1 John 1:6-9).[3]

### Reunion with God Provides a Rationale for the Deity of Christ

Presenting salvation in this way can also provide a rationale for the deity of Christ, which, as I explained in chapter 4, is the most common Muslim objection to the gospel. One of the mistakes we make when we teach Christ's deity to the Muslim is that we simply assert that it is so "because Jesus or Paul said so." Muslims, however, counter this with equally direct and logical Qur'anic propositions. We often fail to demonstrate *why* our Savior had to himself be God if he was to accomplish our salvation.

When we do talk about salvation, we explain that Christ had to die for us because we are guilty and need forgiveness, and someone who was not guilty had to take our place. But that begs a question: *Why would that substitute have to be divine?*

However, if salvation is depicted as the *reunion* of God and man, then the One bringing them together in one body would himself have to be both God and man. Athanasius, Irenaeus, Gregory of Nazianzus, and a number of other Church Fathers spoke of man's problem in these terms. Rather than simply talking about our sin debt, they maintained that we had been separated from God and needed to be reunited. The incarnation, death and resurrection of Christ were the necessary elements to reunite man to God.[4]

What about the problems Muslims have with God "becoming" man? Muslims already have a concept of God being "embodied" in something in how they think about the Qur'an.[5] Most Muslims see the Qur'an as a divine book that enables a type of "communion" or "connection" between the believer and Allah. Experiencing the Qur'an is a way, most Muslims believe, of *experiencing* God.

Jesus is that true Divine Word, the embodiment of God.[6] In experiencing him, we experience God. This is how many of the earliest Christian theologians talked about Jesus. They said that in the Godhead the Father functions like the mind, Jesus like a word spoken by that mind, and the

Spirit like the breath that carries the word to our ear. In the Word and the Spirit, we experience the transcendent God.

When Timothy I of the Nestorians (died 823), who is one of the first Christians on record to debate this issue with Islamic leaders, presented Jesus to Caliph al-Mahdi, he said that Jesus was born of God as a "word was born from the soul," or as "light was born from the sun."[7] Both of these images are biblical analogies (Hebrews 1:3; John 1:1). Just as a man's word is at the same time separate from him and yet still part of him, so the Word of God is in some ways separate from God ("with God") and at the same time fully God. Just as light emanates from the sun, yet seeing the light of the sun is the same as seeing the sun itself, so seeing and experiencing Jesus Christ is experiencing the very essence of God.

Finally, who else but God could overcome death and the powers of corruption in us? The Qur'an says that to God alone "lies the power of life and death" (22:5-6). Could something less than God really overcome the power of death? And would God let some other creature take credit for overcoming the powers of death?

### Union with God Provides the Assurance of Salvation

Finally, the Muslim's union with God through the cleansing work of Christ assures them of the love, acceptance, and security of God for which they yearn.

As mentioned above, Muslims have attempted to cover their spiritual nakedness by rigorous religious observance. By so doing they hope to take away their shame and bridge the gap between themselves and God. The problem with any man-made covering is that it fails to give us the assurance that our shame has actually been taken away. Even with all our religious devotion, we still sense that something is not right between us and God. It is only when God clothes us *with himself* that we gain the assurance we are right with him. It is the Spirit in believers' hearts who gives them the ability to cry, "Abba, Father." We don't doubt God's approval of us, because we *know* him, we commune with him.

Being "clothed with God" provides a different type of assurance than simply saying to a Muslim that because they have accepted Jesus and gotten their sins paid for, God is obligated to "let them in" on Judgment Day. The Muslim dilemma is that they are taught that it is blasphemy to obligate God to anything on Judgment Day, yet they desperately yearn for some sense that they will be accepted by God in heaven. But being clothed with God is a *covenantal, relational* assurance.

When Muslims have been united with God and in their hearts call him "Father," they will *naturally* ask with Paul, "Who could now bring a charge against us? Who can separate us from His love?" (see Romans 8:30-32). He who is now joined to them and at work within them promises never to forsake them. He who has made them his own will complete the good work he has started within them (Hebrews 13:5; Philippians 1:6)!

Assurance is still based, of course, on a divine "promise," but not just a promise that God is obligated to give them something in the future when they die. The promise of eternal life starts with, and is grounded in, God's relationship with them in the *present*.

In other words, *God's presence in them now guarantees his future with them.* Being clothed with the perfect love and presence of the Father in the present drives out the fear of judgment in the future.

This security is a powerful incentive for Muslims to come to Christ, for Muslims crave the love of their heavenly *Father*. Emir and Ergun Caner, two brothers who converted from Islam to Christianity, say that what Islam most lacked, and what Christianity offered to them, was "the promise of life everlasting."[8] Muslims can find it through God as they are relationally *united* to him in Christ.

### The Approval of God Takes Away Shame

As noted in chapter 5, the early Church Fathers taught that it was being clothed with the love and acceptance of God that kept Adam and Eve from feeling shame over their nakedness. It is only being restored to the love and acceptance of God that can remove our sense of shame.

The reason Muslims are so driven to seek the honor that comes from others is because, as naked souls, they are missing the honor that comes from being approved and accepted by God. The loss of God's approval has left a void they desperately try to fill with the admiration and respect of the ummah (community). They try and replace the honor and esteem they once had in God with honor and esteem that comes from men.

Maintaining honor has caused some of the bitterest pain within Muslim families. Many have been driven away from their homes and communities because they failed morally. I've noted previously that many Muslims have felt compelled to put away or even kill their own children because they depended on the honor of others to "live." Many (if not most) Muslims live in fear of their sins, or the sins of those they love, being discovered, resulting in their loss of honor and being driven into isolation.

Only the love and acceptance of God can reduce that dependence on receiving honor from others. Only the gospel can take away shame and fear. Only being cleansed and clothed by the gospel can bring healing to torn Muslim families.

## 2. Victory

### *The Gospel as Victory over the Power of Sin and Death*

We've seen that Muslims have a problem with the weakness displayed in Jesus' death. Muslims and Christians agree, however, that only God has the power of resurrection (Qur'an 22:5-6). Thus, why not make the resurrection a key element in our presentation of the gospel? Why not present the weakness of the cross as a step toward God's victory over sin and death?

The humiliation of the cross was, you see, part of the *victory* of the resurrection. In Christ's death God destroyed the enemies of life and of His purposes for His creation. When Christ was resurrected, the victorious work of renewal started in us. Resurrection was not just an addendum to Christ's work, but its goal (see Romans 7:24-25; Galatians 2:20).

When the apostles talked about Christ's work, they presented the cross in light of the subsequent resurrection. In fact, it was not "cross" that Luke used as his one-word summary of the apostles' message, but "resurrection" (Acts 1:22; 4:2,33; 17:18; 24:21). New Testament scholar N.T. Wright goes so far as to say that "resurrection" sums up the entire biblical presentation of salvation.[9]

---

Why not make the resurrection a key element
in our presentation of the gospel? Why not
present the weakness of the cross as a step
toward God's victory over sin and death?

---

The early church fathers also emphasized the resurrection in their presentations of salvation.[10] Irenaeus answered the question "For what purpose did Christ descend from heaven?" with the words "That He might *destroy* sin, *overcome* death, and *give life* to man."[11] Notice that the words he used to describe Christ's work are words of power and victory!

Unfortunately, the resurrection often plays little or no role in Western presentations of salvation. It gets added as a historical footnote, a miracle that only proved Jesus really was who he said he was or that the cross had "worked."

The resurrection, however, was the whole goal of Christ's work. The resurrection demonstrates that God is the victorious one, the sole possessor of life, and the only conqueror of the grave. Jesus died on the cross to make the resurrection possible.

Presenting salvation in this way *broadens* the appeal of the gospel to Muslims, as it is based on something other than a justice system that Muslims are explicitly taught to reject.

### Christ as the Victorious and Worthy Intercessor Muslims Seek

Chapter 5 showed how Muslims search for someone who can effectively intercede with God for them. The vast system of intermediaries and intercessors present in folk Islam demonstrates that Muslims are desperate to find someone who can help their troubled, fearful consciences before God.

Christ demonstrated that he, and he alone, has the power to intercede for us (Mark 2:1-12; John 11:38-44). He is the worthy intercessor for whose sake God forgives Muslims' sin and guarantees their blessing. Their faithful intercessor is not a fellow sinner circling a black rock in a desert, but one who lived perfectly, earning the Father's full approval, and who is now seated at the right hand of God pleading the case of his people (Isaiah 53:11; Hebrews 7:25–8:1).

Christ's protection of us also removes us from the curse and control of the powers of evil, which Muslims so greatly fear. To the Muslim, the Christian gospel offers deliverance from all fear, by placing Christ, the source of *baraka* (Arabic, "blessing"),[12] *within* the heart of the believer. First John was written to a group of people steeped in superstition and frightened by the powers of evil, and John assured them that, in Christ, they could stand confident knowing that "greater is he who is in you than he who is in the world" (1 John 4:4 NIV). With Almighty God living inside of the Muslim, he does not need to seek deliverance or help from anyone or anything lesser.

### The Gospel Establishes that God Truly Has No Partners

As noted, five times a day (during their prayers), faithful Muslims reiterate that God has no partners. They understand that God stands, and acts, alone.

It is the gospel, however, not Islam, that most fully demonstrates this. In Isaiah 43:11 God says, "I am the LORD, and *besides Me there is no savior*." Of all the world religions, the Christian gospel alone insists that salvation is entirely of God. Our salvation, the gospel teaches, was not something in which we could partner with God. He became man and saved us *by Himself*, living the life we should have lived and dying the death we were condemned to die. From start to finish, our salvation was the work of a God with no partners. In heaven, our anthem will be "Salvation belongs *to our God*" (Revelation 7:10), and no man will have *any* reason to boast (Ephesians 2:9).

The gospel allows no partners to God in salvation. There is a beautiful picture of this in the Old Testament. Under the Levitical system, in order for a sacrifice to be effective, three things had to be present: the sacrifice, the priest, and God. The priest was to eat part of the sacrifice, showing he was ingesting the punishment of the people into his own body (Leviticus 10:17). When Jesus Christ died on the cross, he played the role of all three. He was the sacrifice being offered, the priest who presented the offering (having taken it into his body), and the God who received it. The *gospel* exemplifies what Muslims believe: "God has no partners." He alone can save, with no help from anyone or anything.

To try and make salvation partially dependent on our own good works is to try and be a "partner" to God. Two priests, Nadab and Abihu, were "struck down before the LORD" for mixing in their own elements in God's prescribed offering (Leviticus 10:3-5). They were trying to "partner" with God and were punished by death.

We agree with Muslims that God has no partners, and this is why we believe the gospel.

### The Gospel Exalts God

Because the gospel demonstrates that only God can save, it exalts God in a way that Islam cannot. The cross, even in its humility and shame, was a mighty act of power and deliverance that gives God unique glory. The gospel is the perfect fulfillment of the Islamic belief that God alone should be exalted.

Whenever God saved in the Bible, it was to display his power and attributes:

- *Psalm 106:7-8:* "Our fathers, when they were in Egypt…did not remember the abundance of thy steadfast love, but rebelled at the Red Sea. Yet he saved them for his name's sake, that he might make known his mighty power" (RSV).

- *1 Samuel 12:22:* "The LORD will not forsake His people, for His great name's sake."

- *Isaiah 48:9,11:* "For my name's sake I defer my anger, for the sake of my praise I restrain it for you…For my own sake, for my own sake, I do it, for how should my name be profaned? My glory I will not give to another" (RSV).

- *Ezekiel 36:22-23:* "Thus says the Lord GOD: It is not for your sake, O house of Israel, that I am about to act, but for the sake of my holy name…And I will vindicate the holiness of my great name… and the nations will know that I am the LORD" (RSV).

Romans 3:24-25 says that in the cross God was able to display both his righteousness and his mercy without compromising either!

Philippians 2:5-11 explains that God glorified himself by doing what no man would ever have done in God's place—he humbled himself and died for those who scorned and rejected him. When a subject rebels against a king, the king shows his power by utter destruction of the subject. Yet when God wanted to show his power over his enemies, he took the form of the lowest of men, lived as a servant, and died an unjust, scorned death. As the Church Father Gregory of Nazianzus once said, "The strength of a flame is demonstrated by its ability to burn downward."

God showed his greatness by his willingness to die in our place. So when Jesus then rose victorious from the grave, Paul says that God in Jesus was given the most glorious name, a name that is above every other name. God's actions in Jesus, Paul says, redound to "the glory of God the Father." Every time a believer calls God "Father" he confesses that the relationship he enjoys with God is the result of God's actions, not his own.[13] In other words, when the King will die for the subject, it says more about the King than it does the subject. It is in the gospel that God's power and glory are most clearly shown.

This angle of the gospel really hit home with some of my Muslim friends.

Once, when teaching an English class of Muslim friends, I told them this story.

> An ancient king had the reputation among his countrymen as being the fairest and most loving king that had ever lived. One day he discovered that money was being stolen from his treasury. He made a decree that whoever was caught stealing from his treasury would be whipped with ten lashes. Several weeks passed by. The king declared that money was continuing to be stolen from his treasury, so he was upping the penalty to twenty lashes. Several more weeks passed by, and money continued to be stolen. The king once again doubled the penalty to forty lashes, which was, in essence, the death penalty.
>
> Two days after this final declaration the thief was caught. It was the king's mother. What was the king to do? Some people thought the king would punish her, but others asked, "How can the most loving king who ever lived kill his own mother?" Some thought that such a loving king would surely pardon his mother, but others contended that this would not be fair. The punishment had been declared. If the king was fair, he must give the punishment.
>
> The king decided that because the law was clear, the punishment had to be given. The king's mother was tied up, the back of her shirt was ripped open, and the guard raised his whip to bring down the first lash. Just before the lash was brought down across his mother's back , the king said, "Stop." The king walked over, took off his own shirt, and wrapped his whole body around his mother's. He looked at the guard and said, "Now hit her."
>
> The guard objected that he could not strike the king's mother without striking the king. The king said, "I am the king, and I am giving you an order. Give her the punishment." And as the guard administered the forty lashes, the king shielded, by his body, every lash from his mother.

When I finished telling this story, one friend responded, "No ruler in our country would ever do this. This king must have been a wonderful king."

The gospel shows God's greatness by his ability, and willingness, to become man and overcome sin on our behalf.

### God's Victory in the Gospel Moves Us to Freely Surrender, to Worship, and to Love Him

The gospel creates a love for God that no other religion can compel: a love in response to God's great beauty, a love that springs from gratitude and adoration.

Islamic theologian al-Faruqi states that the purest heart before God is one in which "God is the sole occupant after all (offensive) objects are removed and banished."[14] *Why then would Allah, who refuses to have "partners," allow his people to hope in and adore anyone other than himself as their Savior?* God wants the praise and adoration that comes from being the only One capable to save!

It is *only* when we know God in this way that we can truly love him. When we serve and obey God because we fear his judgment, we are not loving him, but protecting ourselves. Obeying God is simply a means to an end. We love not him, but what he gives us if we obey, and we fear what he does to us if we do not. As Martin Luther said, we end up resenting a God like that more than loving him. But when we understand the steadfast love that God has promised to us, love in our heart for him grows in response. As 1 John 4:19 says, "We love Him because He first loved us."

What I'm saying is this: Muslims understand that loving God is the greatest of all commandments, but *only the gospel gives them the power to actually do that.*

In many ways, I see Muslims as very similar to the woman Jesus encountered in John 4. She had part of God's truth. She shared a common heritage with the Jews. On the outside, she was very religious and quick to defend her religion. But Jesus realizes that her fervent worship of God is not "in spirit and in truth." The woman, for all her religion, is afraid of God, hiding from him, afraid to be exposed. In fact, her outward religion merely cloaks a heart consumed with sin. It is only when this woman comes out from hiding and acknowledges the truth about herself that she can know and love God in her spirit.

God is not one who wants to be simply obeyed and feared, and he is not one who is satisfied with outward acts of conformity. God wants to be known and loved "in the spirit." When we see that we are "safe," even when completely exposed in God's presence, we overflow with grateful love toward God.

## 3. Story

Presenting the gospel by telling a succession of stories about the prophets avoids some of the obstacles that reasoning through the formula of the "Four Spiritual Laws" encounters.

Syllogisms (deductive reasoning) and God just don't mesh well in the Muslim mind. Trying to show that our logic about the nature of God is superior to theirs may not be nearly as effective as showing them how all the stories of the Bible point to Jesus. Quoting proof-texts from the Bible that prove our position will probably not be very effective either, as Muslims will likely just quote back equally dogmatic verses from the Qur'an that contradict the verses we give. Better is to show how the Bible really tells one continuous story—God keeping his promise to save mankind by coming in Jesus Christ to die for our sins and begin a new creation.

---

In the places around the world where Muslims are coming to believe in Jesus, it is happening, in large part, through...small Bible-study groups.

---

One of the things that really helps the storying approach is that many Muslims are already curious about the prophets spoken of in the Qur'an. The stories of the prophets in the Qur'an are very incomplete. It does not go into much detail about the prophets' lives or messages. In fact, it instructs Muslims to consult the "people of the Book (that's Christians!)" for clarification on the details of the lives of the prophets (5:68-69, 10:94)!

Other Muslims will be open to studying the Bible simply out of curiosity about Western culture or as a way to improve their English.

"Storying" through the Bible also creates a natural support group for Muslims who become Christians. Even if the individual members did not previously know each other, they often develop a trust for one another as they journey together through the Bible. It is recorded that often a whole Bible study group will come to faith at once! As I noted earlier, some missions strategists say, "It is more effective to group people and win them (together) than it is to win them (individually) and group them."[15]

It seems that in the places around the world where Muslims are coming to believe in Jesus, it is happening, in large part, through these small Bible-study groups. A good friend serving as a church planter in Central Asia told me this story:

### The power of the story of the Bible

For two years I taught in the university system of a predominantly Muslim republic in Central Asia, and while there began to interact with Muslims from all over the world, including Pakistanis, Turks, and Arabs.

Most of my evenings were spent, over dinner, in dialogue about Islam and Christianity. Usually, the conversation consisted of their attempts to convert me to Islam. Often this took the form of accusations against Christianity. These accusations generally centered on the doctrines of the Trinity, the Incarnation, and the Atonement. I tried answering their questions in straightforward propositional manner, theologically and philosophically. However, I felt as though my words and categories of thought were alien to them. I kept finding myself thinking, *But if you would just read the Scriptures, you would understand. If you understood the "big story," you would understand the details.* What I needed was a way of answering their questions that allowed them to see the "big picture," the grand narrative of Scripture.

My attempt to do this came in August of 1999, as I invited several of my friends, mostly Muslims, to a Bible study in my flat in the middle of the city. The Bible study would be a 20-week endeavor, in a Q-&-A format, in which I would assign them a portion of Scripture to read each week, and they would come to the study, prepared to answer questions about that text.

To my surprise, everyone I invited accepted the invitation. All 45 of them. And my flat consisted of only one room! So I divided them into five separate study groups, which met on different evenings of the week. From the very first lesson of the study, they were fascinated by the text of Christian Scripture. They began to enter into the world of Scripture, and to understand the things that I had been trying to explain to them for over a year.

The Bible studies progressed from the Genesis account all the way through the crucifixion and resurrection. I will never forget this—nearing the end of our 20-lesson Bible study, as one of my groups realized that the Christ had resurrected, they spontaneously began to applaud! Many of them had become so absorbed in the story, and it had become so convincing to them, that they found themselves believing. A number of my Muslim friends became believers, out of which a church was planted which continues today.

So, my suggestion is that you make getting into a Bible-study group the "goal" of your relationship with your Muslim friend. Getting them in a place to study the story line of the Bible is better than sharing with them, in one or multiple conversations, the "Four Spiritual Laws." When I first lived in a Muslim country, I thought I needed to share the whole gospel in the first spiritual conversation I had with a Muslim. It was overwhelming for them, and felt pretty awkward on my end. Much better, I believe, to simply aim at creating an interest in studying the Bible. It is as they are studying through the major stories of the Bible that Muslims can most easily encounter the gospel.

There are numerous chronological Bible-storying programs specifically designed for Muslims for you to choose from. Or you could come up with your own. If you do, make sure the stories you choose emphasize these major themes:

- *The centrality of the promise*: The promise of salvation is first given in Genesis 3:15, and the rest of biblical history unfolds and fulfills that promise. How each story plays a part in the development of the drama should be demonstrated.

- *The reunion of God and man*: God is acting in the Bible to restore what Adam and Eve lost in the Garden. The stories of the prophets chronicle God's actions to remove the poison of the curse that separated man from him in the Garden. God walked with righteous men in Genesis, then tabernacled with his nation. Finally, he came to be *with* them as *Immanuel*, and now lives *in* them in the Holy Spirit.

- *That salvation belongs to God*: From the moment man first needed salvation, God has taught man to look to him for it. Indeed, he has taught that it belongs only to Him (Isaiah 43:10-11; Revelation 7:9).

- *The role of God's Word in men's lives*: From the first creation, God's Word has been his instrument of creation and guidance. He reveals, heals, and recreates through that Word. He gives it the highest place of honor.

- *The trustworthiness of God*: It is not a limitation on God when he binds himself to his promise. Rather, *his power is demonstrated in his ability to keep all his promises.* The Scriptures demonstrate over and over that God always keeps His promises.

- *The substitutionary sacrifice*: The substitutionary sacrifice has been a key element of God's relationship to man since Adam and Eve's very first sin. Salvation by substitution is a key theme in many of the Bible's stories and dominates the Old Testament temple imagery.

- *The difference in works-based religion and salvation by faith*: All religions can be characterized as either "I obey, therefore I am accepted" or "I am accepted, therefore I obey." The gospel alone teaches acceptance prior to obedience, with acceptance being based not on our merit but on God's mercy in Christ. (We'll get into this more fully in the next chapter.)

- *The glory of God in salvation*: God has acted in the Bible in a way designed to bring glory to his name. The Scripture often explains that the reason God has acted as he has is to demonstrate his righteousness and his mercy (Romans 3:25-26) to glorify his power (Psalm 106:7-8; Ezekiel 36:22-23).

I hope this chapter has helped you think through how you can best present the gospel in a way your Muslim friend can grasp it. I know this seems like a daunting task, but be encouraged—the Holy Spirit has helped thousands of people, since the time of the apostles, explain the one, unchanging gospel in a way that their hearers could understand. He will help you too.

# 7

# The Gospel Confronts the Ultimate Religion of Works

*Understanding Islam as a
Self-salvation Project*

One of my frustrations when sharing Christ with Muslims was that I had a hard time getting them to *disagree* with me that only God's grace could save us. They certainly disagreed that Jesus died to save us, but when I would say something like, "We all are in desperate need of God's grace," they would say, "That's exactly what we believe." When I would say, "We should depend on God's grace, not our goodness, to get to heaven," they would say, "Yes, even Muhammad needed God's grace. But God is most-forgiving, most-merciful! He will forgive—we can trust in him." It was not until I said, "You must trust in Jesus to get to heaven," that they would disagree. In other words, I couldn't get them to disagree with me about how we are to approach God until I brought up the particulars of Jesus' name.

Islam, however, prescribes an entirely different way of approaching God than does the gospel. Islam is the ultimate religion of "works-righteousness." The gospel is "gift-righteousness." Islam operates according to the principle, "I obey; therefore I will be accepted." The gospel declares, "You are accepted; therefore obey." The Qur'an says, "Those things (that you do) that are good remove those that are evil" (11:114). The gospel says, "To him who does not work, but believes on Him who justifies the ungodly, his faith is accounted for righteousness" (Romans 4:5).

The gospel is unique among all religions in that it teaches our acceptance is not based on anything we *do* but on what Christ has *done* for us. It is not spelled "D-O" or "D-O-N'-T," but "D-O-N-E." It was not until I made that distinction clear, using clear terminology and biblical examples, that I got them to see that Jesus was saying something entirely contradictory to the teaching of Islam. In this chapter, I want to help you develop the ability to do that. I want to help you understand how works-righteousness operates, and how the gospel challenges it.

---

When you make the gospel clear, you can expect one of two strong reactions: enthusiastic embrace, or stringent disagreement.

---

Confronting the religion of works-righteousness is one of the major themes of the New Testament. The religion of works-righteousness was Jesus' most vocal earthly opponent! The gospels are filled with stories of the conflict between Jesus and the "teachers of the law." Ultimately it was the law-teachers who had Jesus killed.

The animosity of the religious toward Jesus is not unique, of course, to first-century Judaism. The natural tendency of the fallen human heart is to seek justification in what we do, in what separates us and makes us better than others. The gospel challenges the entire works-righteousness mind-set, and so those under that system hate the gospel message. When you make the gospel clear, you can expect one of two strong reactions: enthusiastic embrace, or stringent disagreement. If you haven't received one of those two reactions, you haven't made the gospel clear.

To understand how works-righteousness operates, we must go all the way back to the Garden of Eden.

## The Essence of Sin: Idolatry and Self-Salvation

### Sin as Idolatry

The first sin (in the Garden of Eden) was our decision that the fruit of a forbidden tree and the knowledge it promised was more important than the presence and approval of God in our lives. Paul indicates that that original sin was idolatry: They "worshipped and served the creature rather than the Creator" (Romans 1:25). You may ask, "How was Adam and Eve's eating of the forbidden fruit worship? I don't see them bowing down to the tree…"

True, but Adam and Eve worshipped the tree in that they thought possessing it would make them happier than possessing God would. They "worshipped the tree" as an all-satisfying object (rather than God), and thus traded the "glory of the invisible God" for an earthly substitute.

That is the essence of all sin: We substitute something for God, deeming that "thing" more central to our identity than God is. That "thing" takes many forms…money, career achievement, reputation, sexual pleasures, and so on. Whatever "it" is, we believe we cannot live without that thing and will give up anything else for it. That thing becomes a "functional god" to us.

The first effect of our disobedience was a sense of nakedness. Even before they sinned, Adam and Eve were naked…but their nakedness didn't bother them. As I've pointed out earlier, after their sin, they then had a sense of shame about their nakedness. Why did their nakedness now bother them? Prior to their sin Adam and Eve were "clothed" in the love and acceptance of God. Sin stripped them of that and left them (and us as their descendants) with a sense of nakedness—that is, exposure, guilt, and shame. We believe we are not lovable as we are. We feel naked and exposed.

### Religion as Self-Salvation

What did Adam and Eve do about that sense of nakedness? Immediately, Genesis says, they covered themselves with fig leaves. That's what we all do in our lives and is the fuel of all the world's religions. We are on a quest to find that acceptance and satisfaction that we had previously known in the presence of God.

The world religions teach that living according to certain lifestyles or participating in certain rituals will cover our guilt and make us acceptable to God. Religion says, "If you do the right works, you will be righteous." The Qur'an gives (as we discussed in chapter 5) a long and detailed list of how to act, dress, think, and behave. If you follow carefully these instructions, Allah will approve of you and you are more likely to be accepted into eternal bliss.

## Why Works-Righteousness Doesn't Work

### 1. Works-righteousness fails to address the "root" idolatries that drive our sin.

The root of sin is esteeming something to be a more satisfying object of worship than God. Works-righteousness religions, including Islam, fail to address that issue. They simply give you a prescribed set of practices to avoid judgment or inherit blessings. You can "use" religion, or God, to get the thing you want without ever addressing that the root of sin is that you want the "thing" more than you want God himself.

Islam, for example, warns Muslims of the terrors of hell and uses that to motivate Muslims to obey. It promises them the sensual luxuries of heaven if they live righteously. Many Muslims pursue these things without caring for God at all. They are using God. Even a quick perusal of the Qur'an will show that Muhammad used the threat of punishment and promise of sensual reward as the primary motivator for right behavior, not love of or delight in God. Islam is used to obtain things—namely heaven—not God. God's favor is a means to an end. And any end other than God is idolatry.

For many Muslims, religious zeal is a way to earn earthly respect. In Muslim cultures, religious zealots are admired.

The New Testament is full of examples of people who were religiously active, but wholly idolatrous. For example, the "rich young ruler" did not want to leave his money or his worldly stature to follow Jesus. He was "rich" in both material possessions and self-respect, and considered both to be a more valuable possession than Jesus. He wanted Jesus to give him eternal life, but was not willing to leave his "stuff" to possess only Jesus.

The "woman at the well" in John 4:7-24 used doctrine and ritual to avoid really knowing God. Religion was a mask that kept her from knowing God in spirit and in truth.

Love for God is genuine only when God is a means
to nothing else but God. Righteous acts
are righteous only when they are done out of a love for
righteousness and not as a means to anything else.

Perhaps the starkest example of using religion for idolatrous ends is Judas Iscariot. Most New Testament scholars believe that Judas betrayed Jesus because he was disappointed with him. Judas had hoped that the Messiah would reward the righteous (the Jews) and punish the rule breakers (the Gentiles). Judas wanted a Messiah that would give political power back to the Jews and liberate them from Rome. Jesus, however, taught that salvation was first and foremost not deliverance from political bondage to political freedom, but deliverance from the bondage of sin unto knowing

God. Judas wanted a Messiah who would reward "the righteous" with power and money. Jesus taught that he himself was the reward. In a very revealing scene right before he betrays Jesus, Judas is furious because money is being "wasted" on his Rabbi. Throughout his whole religious journey Judas never perceives the value of simply knowing Jesus. Jesus, for Judas, was a means to something else, and never the end itself.

Love for God is genuine only when God is a means to nothing else but God. Righteous acts are righteous only when they are done out of a love for righteousness and not as a means to anything else.

The Qur'an is not an adoring, worshipping love letter about God. It is a guide for what behavior will increase your chances of avoiding hell and earning heaven. Renowned Islamic scholar Abdullah Yusuf Ali notes in his preface to the Qur'an that the Qur'an's central subject is man and what man must *do* to "succeed" in eternal life.[1] Islam never addresses the root of man's sin, that we have substituted some other delight for the place in our hearts only God should have.

Understanding this helped me realize why even people who are morally and religiously fervent (like Muslims) can still be very far from God. When I lived among Muslims, I had trouble understanding why people whose morality and devotion to religion was every bit as high as mine could have "unregenerate hearts." If the mark of God's Spirit was a devotion of the pursuit of righteousness, they seemed to possess even greater marks of regeneration than I did! It was reading Jonathan Edwards' *Religious Affections* that finally helped me to see that "doing righteousness" is no indication of a love for God. Righteousness is only pleasing to God when you do righteousness solely out of love for him and righteousness itself. Good deeds can be wicked in the eyes of God if done for the purpose of merit or as a means to an end. Of course merit, salvation, and reward form the entire foundation on which Islam is built.

The gospel teaches that what we have lost is the love of God, and that God can only be restored to us by giving himself back to us freely in Christ. The gospel offers God back to us, at no cost to us. In light of the beauty of God that we see in the gospel, the love in our hearts for him will naturally grow. As 1 John 4:19 says, "We love Him *because* He first loved us."

## 2. When our acceptance is based on our performance, we merely exacerbate two root sins in our heart: pride and fear.

When we meet a religion's standards of goodness and acceptability, we feel proud and look down on those who don't meet those same standards. At the same time, we live in constant fear that if we don't meet those standards, we will be rejected. Our religious devotion is fueled by our fear of rejection and love of praise. Pride begets more sin, and fear of God does not create love for him, but an anxiety to prove ourselves to him and to others.

Let me use an example I've heard recently: The sin of racism arises, ultimately, out of insecurity. The racist feels the need to look down on other people (in his case, a whole race of people) to bolster his own self-image. If you try to change the racist by saying, "Don't be a racist, because racists are bad people," you are implying to him that bad people will be rejected. And if he wants to avoid rejection, he should conform to the moral behavior that will gain him acceptance. You are appealing to his fear and insecurity—the *very things that prompted the racism to begin with!*

The gospel, on the other hand, attempts to cure the sin of racism not by threatening rejection, but by showing us the unconditional acceptance we have received in the cross. How could those of us who have been accepted by Christ refuse to accept others? This is what happened with the apostle Peter. Peter had some racist tendencies, believing Gentiles to be inferior to Jews. When Paul confronted Peter, he did not threaten him with rejection. Rather, he said, "Peter, you were accepted by Christ when you were an outsider. How could you then refuse to receive other outsiders?"[2] The generosity of the gospel, not fear of rejection, was Peter's catalyst for change.

Peter's whole life is the story of how the gospel cures the fear and pride that religion creates. Peter ran the gamut between pride and fear depending on how well he was doing at the moment. When Peter realized who Jesus was (Luke 5:8), he was so overwhelmed with a sense of his own moral failure that he said, fearfully, "Depart from me, for I am a sinful man!" Later, however, when feeling good about his accomplishments, he proudly boasted to Jesus that "though they all fall away, I will not!" (Mark 14:29-31 RSV).

It was only when Peter understood the gospel that both his fear and pride were taken away. After the worst failure of his life (denying Jesus), he jumps out of the boat to run *toward* Jesus, realizing that Christ had accepted him, through the cross, despite his failures (John 21:7). No longer does his sense of failure cause him to live with a fear of rejection. Understanding the gospel also drove out Peter's need for pride. Jesus asked him, "Peter, do you still say you love me *more* than the other disciples love me?" (That is, "Do you still think you'll be faithful to me more than the other disciples?") Peter responds simply with "You know that I love you," no longer proudly exalting himself above the other disciples (21:15). Peter's sense of God's unconditional acceptance had driven out his need to lift himself above others.

Islamic culture is rife with both pride and fear. Pride is easy to see in the ostentatious rituals of many Muslims, the way shameful elements are hidden in Islamic communities, and in the condemning violence some Muslims commit against outsiders. Fear is present in the heart of even the most ardent Muslims because their status is never sure. Even in the most moderate Islamic texts, you won't find any instruction about how someone can gain the assurance of God's tender affection.[3]

### 3. The insecurity of always wondering if we've done enough to be accepted causes spiritual fatigue and even hatred of God.

When you constantly wonder if you've done enough to be accepted by God, you begin to resent the God that threatens you with punishment. Outwardly you may continue to boldly attest to your love for him, and you may even convince yourself that you love him. But inwardly, you rage against the God who "enslaves" you. As the wickedness of your heart surges inside of you, you begin to resent the God who makes you act contrary to your heart's desires and holds you captive only by his power to throw you into hell.

The apostle Paul was a great example of a religiously zealous man who hated God. Paul said of himself that, though zealous for the law, he could not keep his heart from coveting. The commandment of God to "not covet" only exacerbated his desires, stoking the power of sin. He says in Romans 7:10, "The very commandment which promised life proved to be death to me" (RSV). In other words, the commands did not increase his love for God, but stoked his resentment of God.

In 1 Corinthians 13:1-4 Paul speaks of people (like he once was) who are zealous in religion, giving even their own bodies to be burned in sacrifice. But for all their devotion, they cannot produce an ounce of love in their hearts for God. Without the love of God, Paul says, all religious devotion is "worthless."

Such a description, I believe, matches Muslims perfectly. They live with the understanding that after living the best life they can, they must still walk the tightrope of God's judgment, unsure if their goodness is sufficient to carry them to heaven. This produces fear, fatigue, and resentment of God. You cannot really love someone you fear rejects you.

Only the gospel of God's perfect, unconditional love for us can create a *real* love in our hearts for him. Realizing how much God has loved us, we begin to delight in him. His love for us begins to overflow in us toward others. We begin to serve others not as a way to gain favor from God, but because we know that we have it. We don't do religious, moral, or "loving" things because we *have to*, but because we *want to*. Our love for God and others is a response to his love in us! Love *from* him produces love *for* him. Love begets love. It is God's "complete love" that drives out fear, "for fear has to do with punishment," and whoever fears has not been completed in God's love (see 1 John 4:18).

---

Religious devotion may trim down the fruits of sin,
but only the love of Jesus can pull up the roots.

---

From there, the overwhelming, all-satisfying love of God in the gospel will drive out our other sinful desires. Paul said in Titus 2:11 that it was the "grace of God" that taught us to deny "ungodliness and worldly passions" (NIV). In Galatians 5:16 he says that it is walking in the Spirit (by believing the gospel—Galatians 3:2) that enables us to "not fulfill the lust of the flesh." Our assurance of the love of God becomes the basis of our growth in spiritual maturity.

As the Puritan John Owen once said, religious devotion may trim down the fruits of sin, but only the love of Jesus can pull up the roots.

### Examples of Jesus Confronting Works-Righteousness

In the following accounts in the Gospels, Jesus confronts the works-righteousness of the Jews. These stories have particular relevance to Muslims:

*In Luke 18:9-14, Jesus tells the story of two men who went to the temple, a tax collector and a Pharisee.* The tax collector, one of those citizens known for their immorality, stands at the back of the temple weeping over his sin and unable to lift even his eyes to God. The Pharisee, a man of impeccable moral repute, stands at the front of the temple, confident in his stellar record of achievement. Which man, Jesus asks, went home righteous? His answer is revolutionary for the Muslim: The man *at the back* with no record to stand on. Why? The Pharisee came before God with his own righteousness. He also left with his own righteousness, a righteousness unable to please God. The tax collector came in with no righteousness, and grasped the righteousness of God available by faith. The righteousness God accepts is not a righteousness we earn, but one he gives.

***Matthew 19:16-30 records the story of a rich young ruler who came to Jesus seeking eternal life.*** The young man is described as rich in both personal accomplishment and moral rectitude. Jesus turns this young, successful, religious man away because he treasures his money too much to treasure God, and his own righteousness too much to humbly receive God's righteousness. Coming to God, this story teaches us, means repenting not only of our sin, but also of our "righteousness."

***John 8:1-11 recounts how Jesus reacted to an immensely immoral woman, caught in the very act of adultery.*** Such a woman would be subject to death both in Israel and in most Muslim countries. Jesus' reaction to her is to say, "Neither do I condemn you; go and sin no more." Muslims would reverse the order of those clauses, as would most religious people: "Go and sin no more, and I will not condemn you." But with Jesus, obedience flows from acceptance, not toward it.

***In Luke 8:40-48, a woman with an "issue of blood" approaches Jesus,*** an incident we've examined previously. This woman would have been ceremonially unclean and would need to purify herself before coming before God or a holy man. Muslims react with horror when she reaches out her hand to touch Jesus. One who is defiled should not pollute the Holy One! Jesus' response is entirely unexpected, however. He calls her "daughter" and tells her that her faith has made her well. With Jesus, cleanliness is not the path to touching God; touching God is the path to cleanliness. When the unholy touches the holy, the unholy does not defile the holy; the holy purifies the unholy. God's holiness is saturated with redeeming love.

***In Mark 7:24-30, a Gentile woman approaches Jesus, seeking healing for her daughter.*** Jesus responds by calling her a "dog." Undaunted, she says, "But even the dogs get to eat what falls from the master's table." Her expectation was that Jesus would reward her not because of her amount of goodness, for she was, truly, just a "dog," but because of the amount of grace in his heart, which overflowed from the table enough to take care of a dog like her. It is not the worthy who receive the favor of God, but those who put their hope in his kindness.

*Jesus' story of the unforgiving servant in Matthew 18:21-35 confronts those religious people who cannot forgive others,* showing that for all of their religion they are still children of hell. Because Muslims believe that people are rewarded according to their goodness, they bear a real disdain for those who fail to live up to the ideals of Islam. Why can the servant in Jesus' parable not bring himself to forgive? Because he has no concept of how much he's been forgiven of. It is God's forgiveness, not our righteousness, which creates compassion for others.

*Jesus' most famous parable, the parable of the prodigal sons (Luke 15:11-32), has a profound meaning for Muslims.* The parable presents two lost sons, one irreligious and the other religious. Muslims have no trouble seeing the first son, who shames the father by leaving for a life of raucous living, as a bad sinner. But Jesus presents a second prodigal son in the story, the son who stays home. This son, for all his goodness, is also not interested in the father. Like the younger son, he is interested only in what the father can give to him. He is angry when he sees the father happy and when the father gives some of his inheritance to the returning son. He shows his estrangement from the father by his inability to show grace. Again, coming to God means not only repenting of our sin, but repenting of our false sense of righteousness, which leads to pride and apathy toward others.

*In Matthew 23, Jesus utters the seven woes over the religion of the Pharisees.* These woes serve as God's description and condemnation of works-righteousness religion for all time. These distinctions between works-religion and the gospel all arise from whether or not we see our salvation as something we earned or something given to us by God. It would be helpful to study these characteristics of religion with the Muslim.

## Confronting the Works-Righteousness of Muslims

When we explain the gospel to a Muslim, we must make clear that it teaches an entirely different way of approaching God than Islam does. Salvation, the gospel teaches, is entirely the gift of God, given freely by his grace and accomplished entirely by him for us. Again, there are only two kinds of religions: those that teach you to obey in order to be accepted; and those that teach that you obey because you are accepted.

In every story you share from the Bible, show how God confronts attempts at self-salvation. He rejects Adam and Eve's fig leaves and clothes their nakedness himself. He tears down the tower of Babel to build a great nation, instead, from a sterile old man. He refuses to heal the mighty Naaman in exchange for great payment, but instead makes Naaman dip seven times in the piddly waters of the Jordan.

We must look for opportunities to explain that our "religious devotion" is done in *response* to God's grace, not to earn it. When I lived in a Muslim context, I felt a great temptation to show them that I did many of the very same things that they did, and that Christians are just as righteous as they are. I wanted to show that we also fasted, prayed, gave generously, and took Scripture memorization seriously. But never forget that, if you are saved by faith in Christ, your reasons for doing these things are entirely different from those of Muslims. You do not want to convey to them that you are fervent in your religion for the same reasons they are fervent in theirs.

I have heard of Christian missionaries who refuse to fast along with the Muslims in Ramadan because they do not want Muslims to think that they also are trying to earn their salvation. They fast throughout the year, but for entirely different reasons, and so try to distinguish their fasts and prayers from those that Muslims do. When asked why they are not fasting or praying as the Muslims do, they explain that what they do is in response to God's approval, not in order to earn it. Their "works" are of a fundamentally different nature.

The gospel of grace stands in complete contrast to the works-righteousness of Islam. This theme must be dominant in our testimony to Muslims and in our explanations of the Bible and why we live our lives as we do. We must continually come back to this theme: The gospel is what God did for us in Christ that we could not do for ourselves. Forgiving love and delight in God, not just fervent obedience, are the signs of a changed heart responding to the gospel's grace. When we do this, the stark difference between the gospel of Jesus and the works-based religion of Muhammad will be seen.

8

# The Objections, Part One
*About God, Jesus, and the Cross*

When you are explaining the gospel to a Muslim, a routine set of objections surface. My goal here is not to deal exhaustively with every objection that will come up, only the primary ones that inevitably surface when Muslims study the Bible. After explaining the objection, I'll provide you with a way to navigate through them or around them—so you can get back to studying the gospel story with the Muslim.[1]

## "Belief in the Trinity Is *Shirk*"

The Trinity is by far the most common and most immediate objection of Muslims to Christianity. Muslims believe that Christians worship three Gods, which makes them guilty of *shirk,* the worst of all possible sins. They also are taught that Christians believe that the birth of Jesus was the result of a sexual encounter between God and Mary. Muslims find the doctrine of the Trinity both blasphemous and offensive. In addition to that, Muslim clerics often instruct their people that the doctrine of the Trinity is inherently illogical! How could 1+1+1 still equal 1? Furthermore, Muslims see the complexity of the Trinity as proof that it is not of God. God's truth, they believe, is simple. The Trinity is too complex to be true.

There are three primary ways you can deal with this objection.

### 1. You can address the question of illogicality head-on.

If you take this approach you must first be clear as to what Christians are actually saying about the Trinity. The Trinity is not a family of three Gods.

The Trinity is not a *triplex* (1+1+1=3), but a *tri-unity* (analogously, 1x1x1=1). As Norman Geisler and Abdul Saleeb observe,

> His one essence has multiple "personalities." Thus, there is no more of a mathematical problem in conceiving the Trinity than there is in understanding 1 to the third power ($1^3$).[2]

The Trinity is the belief that God eternally exists in three persons—Father, Son, and Spirit. None of the persons had a beginning or is "more God" than the others. And of course, no orthodox Christians have ever believed that God had sex with Mary or that Jesus was the offspring of sexual intercourse.

***Helpful analogies.*** Christians do believe that Jesus is the "Son" of God, however, and the Qur'an denies that God could beget a son ("He is neither begotten nor begets"—sura 112). *Son,* however, does not have to mean offspring in the biological sense. Most languages have some instance where *son* is used analogously. For example, in the Malay language, a key is called a "son of the lock." The Bible also speaks about the nature of God to us analogously, in ways we can understand. The relationship that human fathers have with their sons *in some ways* resembles the relationship *the* Father has with *the* Son. (Any analogy can be pushed further than the author intends to imply things the author did not mean.)

---

Biblical analogies...are good places to start, for they depict the oneness of God existing in multiple "Persons."

---

For the Muslim, speaking of Jesus as the "Word" (as the apostle John does) might be easier to understand, at first, than speaking of him as the "Son." First, Muslims are familiar with the title "Word" for Jesus, as the Qur'an calls Jesus just that in 4:171. The "Word" is also the one-word descriptor of Jesus in the listing of the 25 prophets. It also makes for a less cumbersome analogy. Just as a man's spoken word is, in some sense, separate from him, and in another sense, part of him, so is Christ, the Word of God, both separate from God and at the same time God. As I noted earlier, some of the earliest Christians explained that the Father is like the mind that conceives the thought, the Word is the expression of that thought, and the Spirit is the voice that carries the thought along. All three are separate in person but in essence one.

*The Objections, Part One* | 107

Another biblical analogy for the Trinity is used in Hebrews 1:3: "The Son is the radiance of God's glory." Just as the one sun emits light, heat, and radioactive waves, and by encountering any of those you experience the sun itself, so in encountering Jesus you experience the very essence of God. It would make little sense to say, "I see the light from the sun, but I do not see the sun." They are one and the same. The same is true for the Son of God and God.

These two analogies, those of "word" and "radiance," like all analogies, will break down if pushed far enough. They are certainly better, however, than the ones Western Christians often use, such as water being able to exist in the forms of ice, liquid, and gas or the egg being the yolk, the white, and the shell. "Word" and "light" are biblical analogies, and they are good places to start, for they depict the oneness of God existing in multiple "Persons."

***The issue of complexity.*** Muslims assert that because the Trinity is a complex doctrine it cannot be true. Why? In what other science is the simplest explanation always the correct one? Believing that the stork brings new babies may be easier than believing the complex processes of conception and gestation, but that does not make it true. In fact, when you consider that the concept of the Trinity arose from a fiercely monotheistic Jewish context, its complexity and incredibility argue *for* its truthfulness! Why would a band of devoted Jews, who were historically and dogmatically monotheistic, interject a "Son of God" into their beliefs about God if it were not necessitated by Jesus himself? The Jews who first spoke of the Trinity were as committed to their monotheism as are Muslims today. This is not a doctrine they would have invented for their convenience!

The difficulties we have in grasping the Trinity result from our limitations as humans, not from contradictions in the nature of God. A French theologian in the nineteenth century once told a parable about a three-dimensional, spherical god who wanted to reveal himself to his two-dimensional creations, who existed as dots on a page. To do this, the spherical god passed through the two-dimensional plane. The dots watched in amazement as the god-sphere passing through the plane, started as a dot, slowly expanded, and then gradually shrank again to a dot. The poor dots were bewildered and argued over whether or not god was a circle or a dot, for surely he could not be both. Yet they had seen him as both a dot and a circle! If this is the difficulty a two-dimensional creature would have with a three-dimensional god, how much greater must be our difficulty with an infinite God!

Muhammad himself said that speculation about the nature of God is futile. Thus, even Muhammad would seem to warn us against making absolute declarations about what God's nature must be like (as in, "because he is one he cannot be a Trinity") are improper!

You can certainly "win" in regard to the logicality of the Trinity argument. However, the *core* reason Muslims do not accept the Trinity is that they have been told in dogmatic, propositional terms that the doctrine is blasphemous. Therefore, using this first method, even if you offer the most persuasive logical reasoning, is unlikely to convince them. There are two better ways of approaching the Trinity, given to us by the early church and the pattern of Scripture itself.

*2. You can (as the Church Fathers did) demonstrate how the only way men could be saved is for God to have become man.*

Muslims reject the Trinity because they do not see why God had to become man to save us. Here we can learn from the early church. In his famous *De Incarnationi Verbi Dei* (*Why God Became Man*), Athanasius demonstrated that because man's chief problem was separation from God, God overcame that by reuniting himself to man. The Scriptures reveal a God coming to live "among" people. The presence of God dwelt in the holy of holies in the temple. When Jesus shows up on the scene he claims to be the *new* temple. The apostle Paul taught that those who are now "in Christ" are literally joined to God.

As we discussed in chapter 6, showing Muslims why God had to become man to save us and why only God could have saved us will make it easier for them to grasp that Jesus is indeed God.

*3. You can follow the pattern of the Scriptures and let the doctrine of the Trinity unfold progressively during a chronological study of the Bible.*

The Jews were a stringently monotheistic people. How did a set of sincere Jews come to embrace the Trinity? Neither Jesus nor the apostles argued for it propositionally...that is, none of them said, "God is a Trinity, which means he is both one and three. Here are some analogies for that." Instead, the Scriptures presented God as one, then Jesus as God and yet somehow distinct from God the Father, and then let the doctrine of the Trinity emerge out of that.

The Old Testament is birthed in repeated affirmations of the oneness of God. This was the unique message Israel was to carry to the Canaanite nations. The Scriptures all along, however, hint at God's tri-unity. For example, God refers to himself as "us" in Genesis 1:27; he uses the plural word for "one" (Hebrew, *ehad*) in the great declaration of Jewish monotheism, "The LORD is one" (Deuteronomy 6:4); and he speaks of himself as distinct from his Spirit in Isaiah 48:16. As you study the Old Testament with a Muslim, leave this tension unresolved, as the Scripture does, until Jesus shows up on the scene. Let Muslims observe Jesus doing things God alone can do, receiving worship, and calling himself God. They will struggle with the deity of Christ in the same way the Jews of the first century did, and many will come to the same conclusion Thomas did, which led him to exclaim, "My Lord and my God!" Jesus can prove his own deity. Study his life with a Muslim and let Jesus do it in his own way.

You see, Jesus did not simply walk around claiming outright that he was God, at least not that often. Rather, he *demonstrated* that he was God. He knew the reaction Jews would have to a man claiming to be God, so he challenged them to believe him for the works' sake (see John 14:11). And his works screamed, "I am God!" Jesus' life presents a dilemma that only the doctrine of the Trinity can solve!

In other words, raise the question of the Trinity in the order and to the extent that the Scripture does. When the objections and questions about the Trinity do surface, ask, "What are the Scriptures trying to teach us?"

I also found it helpful to ask, "*Could* God become man if he wanted to?" The answer is almost always yes, since Allah, they believe, can do anything. Then the question becomes "*Did* he?" This frames the question where the Christian can answer it. *Could God become a man, and if so, is there reason to believe that he did?* Another question you might ask is, *If God did become man, what might he look like?*

## Talking points

- Does the Muslim understand what Christians *really* say about the Trinity?

- The biblical analogy of Jesus as the Word of God is a way by which we understand that Jesus was separate from the Father, yet fully God.

- It should not be surprising that finite men find the nature of God baffling.

- The Trinity was involved in the process of salvation, and each member contributes to reversing the effects of the Fall. The Father planned salvation, the Son executed it, the Spirit applies it.

- *Could* God become a man if he wanted to? What would that look like?

- *Always be looking for a chance to ask, "Would you like to study the Bible from beginning to end with me?"*

## "Belief in Penal Substitution Is Immoral and Illogical"

I recommended in chapter 6 that you present the work of Jesus on the cross as cleansing from and victory over sin and death rather than simply as payment of a debt to God. Inevitably, however, at some point the doctrine of penal substitution will have to be discussed and defended. I would suggest offering the following reasoning for it.

### 1. The doctrine of penal substitution has strong biblical support.

Throughout all of the "previously" revealed books (the Torah, the Prophets, the Gospels), penal substitution is central to the biblical message.[3] The idea that Christ satisfied the justice of God is the clear teaching of passages such as Genesis 9:6, Exodus 21:24, Leviticus 1:4 and 17:11, Isaiah 53:5-6, and Hebrews 9:22.

### 2. Penal substitution is necessary for any real forgiveness.

Muslims often ask why we believe God can't forgive as we do. We usually don't require "atonement" or propitiation of our wrath when we forgive someone we love. We simply waive the penalty. Why couldn't God do the same?

However, we can never just waive the consequences of sin. When we forgive, we agree to absorb those consequences. Say a man breaks into your home and steals some money you had set aside to pay your bills. He immediately spends all the money. Later, he comes to you and confesses, and you forgive him. Forgiveness is free for him but costly for you, for what you are agreeing to do is to *yourself* make up the debt incurred by his actions. The bills still need to be paid, and you are agreeing to repay, to yourself, what he has stolen.

What if the "sin" against you was not monetary? What if someone lied about you and ruined your reputation? You can respond to them in one of a few ways. You can make them "pay" for their sin against you by venting your anger on them, or by going back to all the people they lied to and ruining their reputation. But if you choose to forgive them, you are saying to them that you yourself will absorb the consequences of their evil. You will not make them pay, you will not ruin their reputation, and you will not vent your anger. You will "bear in your own body" the bad effects of their sin. They sinned, but you will suffer.

This is precisely what God did with us in Christ. We had robbed the bank of God's justice. God made up what we owed to his account. We had wounded the honor and glory of God. God bore that wound in his own body when he suffered on the cross. We sinned, but God suffered for it, so that we would not have to endure the dreadful consequences of our sin.

God simply will not overlook injustice. Psalm 97:2 says that justice is the inviolable foundation of God's throne, and right must be maintained in the universe. Proverbs 17:15 says, "He who justifies the wicked and he who condemns the righteous are both alike an abomination to the Lord" (RSV). Injustice will be righted. If we suffer the consequences for our sin, it looks like hell. If God suffers the consequences for our sin, it looks like the cross.

### 3. God's own name is at stake.

To simply pass over sin would not only leave wrong unrighted in the universe, it would make a statement about God that is untrue. His name would be demeaned. Jesus died to demonstrate that God is just, and to show that God was just and the merciful justifier of those who put faith in Jesus (Romans 3:25).

### 4. God has to be true to his word.

God declared that the soul that sins would die (Genesis 2:17; Ezekiel 18:20). If he abrogates his promise here, which other promises might he abrogate?

A story I found particularly helpful in teaching this is the account of the Fall of man in Genesis 2–4. (Muslims are curious already about this story, as there is very little detail given in the Qur'an or Hadith.) God's promise to Adam and Eve that the day in which they ate of the fruit they would surely die was very clear.

As the story unfolds, inevitably the question arises, "But what about God's promise?" Ask, "Why didn't they die? Was God wrong? Or was he exaggerating his threats in order to frighten Adam and Eve into submission? Or did he just change his mind?" None of these alternatives are acceptable to the Muslim. One Muslim friend, particularly troubled by this dilemma, responded, "Perhaps their death was inward rather than outward." At this point it was easier to explain what God would have to do to save man. He would have to somehow absorb the death penalty and restore life to us. From here the entire sacrificial system unfolds, starting with the clothing of skins for Adam and Eve, Abel's sacrifice, the substitution of a ram for Abraham's son, and so forth. The promise of death was absorbed in the God-man's innocent death, whose resurrection restores the life that man lost at the Fall.

Also helpful in explaining penal substitution is the story of Abraham's sacrifice of Isaac. Muslims are familiar with that story, believing that Abraham's willingness to offer his son depicts his great submission to Allah.[4] They commemorate the event once a year at *Idul Adha*, one of their major holidays. A bull is sacrificed on behalf of the community.

Once I was invited to go with my neighbors and friends when they went to sacrifice their bull on Idul Adha. I was pushed to the front of the large Muslim crowd as they chanted and cheered. I watched as the imam took the knife and began to cut through the throat of the bull. As blood gushed everywhere, I watched him drop a slip of paper into the blood.

---

It was easy to explain that just as Abraham's son was under a sentence of death, we also are under a sentence of death.

---

As I recalled what the Old Testament sacrifice represented—the death of Christ—I was visibly moved. My neighbor looked at me and said, "Why are their tears in your eyes? It is just a bull."

Later, I asked the gathered family to tell me what the events of the sacrifice represented. They told me that when Allah saw that Abraham was willing to be obedient even to the point of offering his own son, Allah provided an animal to replace his son in sacrifice. The bull represents that replacement. I asked why the imam dropped the names into the blood after severing the neck. They explained that the slip of paper contained the names of those who had purchased the bull for sacrifice, and that dropping their names in the bull's blood credited the merit of that sacrifice to their account.

With this as a backdrop, it was easy to explain that just as Abraham's son was under a sentence of death, we also are under a sentence of death. Just as God provided a substitute for Abraham that would die in his son's place, so God has provided a substitute to die in our place.

### Talking points

- Penal substitution is an established part of prophetic tradition (as in the story of Adam and Eve; the temple; Isaiah 53).

- Penal substitution is the only way God could justly and mercifully deal with sin, thus preserving the honor of his name (Romans 3:25-26).

- Penal substitution is required in order for God not to be a liar (Genesis 2:17).

- Penal substitution is demonstrated in the stories of the prophets, as with Abraham and Isaac (Genesis 22).

### "A Man Cannot Be God"

First, you should heartily agree with this objection. No man can elevate himself to the status of God. This, in fact, is the essence of the first sin (Genesis 3:5)! But the question is not can a man become God, but is God able to become a man? That puts the question on an entirely different footing. From there, I'd proceed like this:

1. Show that our salvation required the special action of God. Only God could overcome sin and death. Only by becoming human could God defeat sin and death and reunite himself to us.

2. Show that Jesus, through his miracles, reversed the effects of the Fall. Who else but God can create, heal, control the weather, and raise the dead?

3. Point out the many places where Jesus claims the titles and

privileges of God, such as his assumption of the name "I AM" (John 8:58); his forgiving of sins (Mark 2:5-7); His reception of worship (John 9:38; 20:28); his claim to be the only Savior (Luke 2:11; John 14:6; see Isaiah 43:11); his claim to share in God's glory (John 17:5-6; see Isaiah 42:8); and his asking people to pray in his name. Jesus claimed to be the new temple (John 2:18-19), which Jews specifically understood to be the place of the very presence of God. Jesus claimed the role of law-giver (Matthew 5–7), a role Jews believed belonged only to God. Other prophets said, "Thus says the LORD," but Jesus would say, "You have heard it said...but *I* say to you." Jesus' claim to divinity was so clear that he was frequently accused of blasphemy and eventually killed for it (Mark 14:61-63; John 8:58-59)!

4. Ask, "*Could* God become man if he wanted to?" Of course, Muslims say—God can do anything. The question then is, "*Did* he?" What do the Holy Books say? What do they predict? The issue is not what we as humans think is or is not possible, but what God says about himself. Muhammad even says that it is blasphemy to argue and speculate about the nature of God. We must believe and obey the revelation regardless of how little it makes sense to us. We are not the judge of God.

5. To note, if you are storying through the Bible and this question comes up early, you may want to determine how quickly you want to answer it. Sometimes it is better to say, "We'll see the answer to this in time. For now, let's stay with what God is teaching through history." At the appropriate time, you can point out how the *works* and *words* of Jesus demonstrate that he is clearly claiming to be God.[5] We can even see in Jesus' own ministry that, at times, he obscured his deity because he knew there were things he would have to teach the Jews before they could grasp his claims to deity! It is only when the Jews saw how perfectly he fulfilled the Old Testament prophecies of salvation that they could grasp that he was indeed God in the flesh! Again, remember that the Jews of Jesus' day were as insistent on the "oneness" of God as Muslims are today!

*Talking points*

- As with the question of the Trinity, ask whether God *could* become a man if he wanted. If so, what would that look like?

- Realize that Muslims may find the incarnation easier to grasp in the context of studying through the Bible. It may be wise to postpone the question and let Scripture reveal this truth in its own time and order.

- Show how in his works and words Jesus is clearly claiming to be God.

## "The Death of Jesus Did Not Really Happen"

Muslims believe that Jesus did not actually die but was replaced mysteriously on the cross by Judas, or by a demon, and God thus had the last laugh. The Qur'an says, "They said (in boast), 'We killed Isa al-Masih (Jesus Christ), the Son of Mary, the Apostle of God,' but they killed him not, nor did they crucify him" (4:157).

To address this, you can certainly argue for the *well-founded historical evidence for the crucifixion.*

1. It is rather tenuous to suggest that the Romans accidentally crucified the wrong person, and that Mary and the other disciples, who knew Jesus intimately, mistook him as well.

2. Medically speaking, it is nearly impossible to claim that the man on the cross did not really die, but only swooned. The water and blood that came from his pierced side were the signs of a ruptured heart.

3. Muslims may claim that God "blinded the eyes of the wicked" so they thought they were crucifying Jesus. But why would God make no distinction between the wicked and his faithful disciples, blinding them all?

4. Would God have allowed Jesus' faithful followers to preach a wildly incorrect "gospel" that fundamentally distorted his work, humiliating him rather than exalting him?

5. If God's purpose in keeping Jesus from dying on the cross was to protect his reputation, didn't he miserably fail? This is as much a complete and total failure of the prophetic ministry of Jesus as Muslims suppose his death to have been!

The real reason Muslims deny the cross is because they neither see the need for it nor believe God would allow one of his prophets to be shamed in such a way. God always vindicates his messengers, they believe, and does not allow them to suffer such humiliation.

> The choice God now presents to the world is whether or not they will believe the world's verdict on God's Prophet (the cross) or God's own verdict (the resurrection).

Therefore, it is most effective to demonstrate from the Old Testament *the need for a substitute*. If Judas had taken Jesus' place, Jesus could not have taken ours! (See the arguments for "penal substitution" above.) Secondly, explain the cross in the context of the resurrection. Explain how the crucifixion was actually part of God's greatest act of power. God *did* vindicate Jesus at the resurrection, and the choice God now presents to the world is whether or not they will believe the world's verdict on God's Prophet (the cross) or God's own verdict (the resurrection). As Muhammad so often said, God is calling people to faith! (See discussion on salvation as "victory," chapter 6).

Finally, it is easy to see why "God revealed" to Muhammad that Jesus did not die and rise again. If the resurrection is true, then how can Muhammad be the "seal of the Prophets"? Why would God need to send Muhammad if the Son of God himself had lived on earth, had died as the final sacrifice, and had risen again to show his power over death?

The fact that Muslims believe Jesus did not die does provide you with one significant benefit, however. It means you *both believe he is still alive*, and as such, can be of help and guidance in the "spiritual journey." I have encouraged many of my Muslim friends to ask him, the only living Prophet, to show himself to them. Many have done just that, and I've seen him answer their prayers in some pretty incredible ways. Three times he showed up to them in some kind of dream! Many others have asked me, even years later, to pray to Jesus for them for help!

*Talking points*

- Remember that most Muslims deny Jesus' death on the cross because they do not understand the need for it. Therefore, take time, through the study of the Scriptures, to establish the need for Christ's death.

- Point out that it is difficult to see how God would have allowed Jesus' faithful followers to make such a grave mistake in spreading the prophet's message.

- Point out that if God's main purpose in keeping Jesus from dying on the cross was to protect his reputation, he miserably failed!

- Explain the death of Jesus in the context of his resurrection. The cross was swallowed up in victory!

- The cross is the world's verdict on Jesus; the resurrection is God's! Which will they believe?

- Encourage them to pray to Jesus, the living Prophet, to ask for help and guidance.

9

# The Objections, Part Two
## About Prophecy, the Bible, and Christianity

### "Moses Predicted Muhammad as the Last Prophet"

Muslims insist that Moses' prediction in Deuteronomy 18:15-17, "The LORD your God will raise up for you a prophet like me" (RSV), refers to Muhammad. They argue that Muhammad was more "like Moses" than Jesus was. Like Moses, Muhammad was married, set up a theocracy, and was a warrior—none of which Jesus did in his lifetime!

How do you answer that? Point out, first, that Moses spoke of a prophet that would arise from "among you, from your brethren" (verse 15 RSV). This would mean the prophet was an Israelite. Sometimes Muslims will contend that "your brethren" refers to the Ishmaelites, since Ishmael was the brother of Isaac. However, Moses uses the same phrase, "among their brethren," in Deuteronomy 18:2, referring to the priests of Israel. (The priests of Israel were obviously Jewish, not Ishmaelites.)

Furthermore, who was *actually* more like Moses—Muhammad or Jesus? The New Testament carefully demonstrates the similarity of Moses and Jesus. The Gospel of John repeatedly raises the question of whether or not Jesus is "that Prophet" that the Jews were anticipating from Moses' prediction, and gives an irrefutable yes (John 1:21,25; 6:14; 7:40; 8:52-53). The Gospel of Matthew walks Jesus through a path nearly identical to that of Moses:

1. Jesus left Nazareth to go to Egypt so he could be called out of Egypt as Israel was (Matthew 2:15; Hosea 11:1).

119

2. The next event Matthew records is Jesus' baptism (Matthew 3:1-17). This parallels Moses' "baptism" in the Red Sea (1 Corinthians 10:2).

3. Jesus then is driven into the wilderness, where he is tempted for 40 days (Matthew 4:1-22), just as Moses and the Israelites were driven into the wilderness where they were tempted for 40 years. (The significant difference, of course, is that whereas Israel wandered for 40 years because of her sin, and Moses was forbidden to enter the Promised Land because of his sin, Jesus was tempted for 40 days *without* sin.)

4. Matthew then declares that Jesus, upon leaving the wilderness temptation, heals "every disease and every infirmity among the people" (Matthew 4:23 RSV). This parallels the name the children of Israel gave to God at Marah, "Jehovah *Rapha*," translated "the God who heals" (Exodus 15:26). In that name they celebrated their deliverance from all the diseases of the Egyptians.

5. In Matthew 5, Jesus goes up to a mountain and gives the people his version of the Law (Matthew 5–7, "You have heard that it was said…but *I* say to you…"), just as Moses had obtained and delivered "his" law from the mountain.

It is Jesus who is "the Prophet" like Moses.

Finally, God's plan of salvation has always come to the world through the Jews. Jesus even declared it so (John 4:22). Every prophet between Abraham and Jesus was Jewish (as Muslims will acknowledge). God told Abraham, Isaac, and Jacob that he had chosen their descendants (the Jews) to bring salvation to the world, and God does not go back on his word.

Perhaps the strongest argument against the assertion that Muhammad is the predicted prophet, however, is to demonstrate how different his message was from that of the other prophets, all of whom preached the gospel of salvation by grace through faith and pointed to the coming of the Messiah. Jesus fulfills the message of those prophets. (This is discussed more below.)

Again, as I've pointed out before, one of the best ways to demonstrate Christ's fulfillment of the message of the prophets is not to argue it (as I have done above), but to let it emerge through the systematic study of stories of the prophets in the Bible.

*Talking points*

- The predicted prophet was to be from "among the brethren" of the Jews.

- Jesus' life paralleled Moses' life, thus making him "like Moses."

- Jesus fulfilled the message of all the prophets.

- Muhammad's message is fundamentally different from that of the other prophets.

## "Muhammad Brought Together the Messages of All the Prophets"

Muslims believe that Muhammad brought together the messages of all the prophets in the Qur'an. Each previous prophet was given a part of the revelation. Muhammad brought them all together, and in reading the Qur'an we get the essence of all the others taught.

The best way to deal with this objection is simply to study the message of the prophets.

### What was the message?

Jesus said that every story told by the prophets really concerned him: "Beginning at Moses and all the Prophets, He expounded to them in all the Scriptures the things concerning Himself" (Luke 24:27). A study of the Scriptures will abundantly demonstrate that claim. Here are some of the things you should be looking for as you study.

The message of the biblical prophets centered on a kingdom, a coming Messiah, a temple with a sacrificial system, God as the Deliverer, and salvation by grace through faith. Sacrifices that atone for sin have been central to revealed religion since the first prophets, as has Israel's hope that a coming Messiah would restore the kingdom to God's people. (Helpful here is that Muslims retain this idea in the name given to Jesus, "Isa al-Masih," *al-Masih* meaning "the sent One.")

The Bible consistently teaches that men are saved not by what they do for God, but by what God has done for them. The Bible teaches trust in God, not performance for God. God rejected Adam's leaf-covering of his own nakedness and provided skins to cover him instead. He provided for Noah an ark of safety in the worldwide flood with one door. He tore down man's attempt to reach him and establish a great kingdom at the Tower of Babel, and instead chose a sterile old man to make his name great in the earth.

---

God...has, from the beginning to the end of revelation, taught his people to look to him for salvation.

---

For Abraham, he provided a ram in the place of Isaac and promised, "I will provide for myself a lamb." He gave a picture of the substitute ram in the sacrificial system of the temple (Leviticus 1:4; 17:11). He said in Isaiah, "I, even I, am the LORD, and besides Me there is no savior" (Isaiah 43:11). Through Jeremiah he said he was "the LORD our righteousness" (Jeremiah 23:6). The anthem song in heaven will be that "salvation belongs to our God" (Revelation 7:10). In other words, God has, from the beginning to the end of revelation, taught his people to look to him for salvation.

The Scriptures demonstrate, as I've indicated previously, that there are really only two religions in the world: the one that says, "I obey, therefore I will be accepted"; and the other that says, "I am accepted by what God has done for me, therefore I will obey." The former has opposed the latter since the day that Cain killed Abel. Salvation by works is the competing message of Islam, completely out of sync with the rest of the Bible. This will become evident as you study the Scripture along with Muslims.

## What was the test of a prophet?

A good question to ask is how God's people were to know that a new prophet, claiming to speak for God, really *was* from God. Simply claiming to speak for God surely is not enough. Even miracles can be faked, and many people have used "miracles" to contradict other "prophets" who also claimed the witness of miracles. Neither is the popularity of a prophet nor the rapid spread of his message proof, for mass movements have happened in many religions throughout history.

*The most important test of a prophet was his congruence with the previous revelations.* If a prophet contradicted the previous prophets, he had to be false, for God's word cannot be changed! Jesus understood this, staking the truthfulness of his message on its congruence with what was already written

(Luke 24:27; John 5:39; 10:34-38). The apostle Peter said that the gospel message he preached was "sure" because it was consistent with what had been revealed centuries before by the prophets (2 Peter 1:18-19). That made his message, Peter said, even "more sure" than hearing a voice from heaven!

*Talking points*

- Invite the Muslim to *study* the prophets with you.

- The central message of the prophets concerned a kingdom, a Messiah, a temple with a sacrificial system, God as the Deliverer, and salvation by grace through faith. The message pointed toward Jesus. Muhammad's message contradicted this message on just about every point. He taught that he was the final prophet, and that we save ourselves by good works.

- Ask, "How were God's people to recognize a true prophet from a false one?" By the congruence of the new prophet's message with the previous ones.

## "The Bible Has Been Changed"

Muslims have an extremely high view of "Scripture." As we saw in chapter 2, they hold the Qur'an in the highest regard, considering its words to be the very words of Allah. Translations of the Qur'an into any other language are considered to be only *interpretations* of the Qur'an, not the Qur'an itself.

They believe the text of the Qur'an abides with Allah in heaven, having forever existed in the past, and forever to be preserved in the future. We cannot change the Qur'an as it exists here because we cannot change it up there! Muhammad received the text of the Qur'an with the command, "Recite!" Allah has declared that he will protect and preserve his word in the Qur'an, and "no change can there ever be in the words of God" (Qur'an 10:64). Even the pronunciation of the words is sacred, since Allah revealed the words in a particular form of Arabic. To suggest that any part of the Qur'an was the result of Muhammad's imagination, or that any part of it has been changed, added to, or lost, is blasphemy.

The other revelations that preceded the Qur'an, the Taurat (Torah), Zabur (David's writings), and Injil (Jesus' gospel), are generally considered to be the writings that now compose the Christian Bible.[1] However, as said previously, most Muslims believe that the "Jewish" and "Christian" holy books have been corrupted. If you show a Muslim that something in the Bible contradicts what the Qur'an says, this is almost certainly how they will respond.

### God protects his Word

I found it helpful to respond to the charge that the Bible had been changed with the same incredulity the Muslim would display if you charged the Qur'an with being changed. Assume the high ground Muslims take with Scripture—that God has sworn to honor and protect his Word. To say that man could change, or do away with, any part of the revealed Word is a challenge to the authority of God himself. These verses from the Old and New Testaments make that clear:

> Forever, O LORD, Your word is settled in heaven (Psalm 119:89).

> My word...goes forth from My mouth; It shall not return to Me void, but it shall accomplish what I please, and it shall prosper in the thing for which I sent it (Isaiah 55:11).

> Assuredly, I say to you, till heaven and earth pass away, one jot or one tittle will by no means pass from the law till all is fulfilled (Matthew 5:18).

Ask the Muslims how they would react if you accused the Qur'an of being changed. They claim that it could not be so, for God's word cannot be changed! And how do they know that? Because the Qur'an promises it! Show them that those same promises were given for the previous holy books as well, *and if God did not honor his promise the first time, they have no guarantee he would honor it the second time.*

### The Qur'an commends the Bible

Furthermore, show him that the Qur'an points its readers to the Bible for clarity on issues of salvation:

> If thou wert in doubt as to what We have revealed unto thee, then ask those who have been reading the Book from before thee. The truth hath indeed come to thee from the Lord: So be in no wise of those in doubt (10:94).

> Let the people of the gospel judge by what God hath revealed therein (5:50).

Nearest among them in love to the Believers (Muslims) wilt thou find those who say "We are Christians," because amongst these are men devoted to learning and men who have renounced the world, and they are not arrogant (5:85).

We believe in God, and in what has been revealed to us and what was revealed to Abraham…and in the Books given to Moses, Jesus and the Prophets, we make no distinction between one and the other (3:84).

Believe in Allah and His Apostle, and the Scripture which He sent to those before him. Any who denieth God, His angels, His books, His apostles, and the Day of Judgment, has gone astray (4:136).

Those who deny God and His apostles, and wish to separate God from His apostles, saying, "We believe in some but reject others," are equally unbelievers (4:150-51).

No change can there be in the Words of God (10:64).

Muslims may respond by saying that these promises apply to the Bible that was in circulation in the time of Muhammad, and that the Bible we have has been so distorted that these instructions and promises no longer apply.

If so, first respond by pointing out that to say that man is capable of changing God's word is an insult to God's authority, as it implies he could not keep the promise he made to protect his word.[2]

Second, point out that the New Testament Muhammad directed Muslims toward is essentially the same one we use today. There are an abundance of manuscripts available today dating from the seventh century or before.[3] *These manuscripts demonstrate that the Bible in circulation at the time of Muhammad was the same Bible we have today.* If the Bible had been changed, it would have to have been centuries prior to Muhammad—which would mean the Qur'an pointed its readers to a flawed, inauthentic source! In other words, if the Bible we use today is faulty, so is the Qur'an's instruction to consult it.

From there, again, you should encourage the Muslim to do as the Qur'an instructs them and read the messages of the previous prophets. Getting them into the Bible is the goal. What Martin Luther said is worth repeating: "The Bible is like a caged lion—when it is attacked, rather than defend it, unleash it!" Don't get bogged down in a "which book is better" debate. You can win that debate, but more important is to get the Muslim into the

Word of God so it can do its own work. Look at the objections not as arguments to be won, but simply as roadblocks to be overcome in getting the Muslim to read the Bible with you.

Remember, since Muslims believe all portions of the Qur'an to be accurate, you can commandeer the passages that affirm the Bible to direct Muslims to read and study it wth you.

*Talking points*

- React with the same incredulity that a Muslim would display if you accused the Qur'an of being changed, pointing out the numerous promises God makes about the preservation of his word.

- Point out that the Qur'an directs its readers to search the Bible for answers.

- Point out that manuscripts of the Bible exist that predate Muhammad's life. These manuscripts demonstrate that the Bible we have today is the same as the one in circulation at the time of Muhammad. If Muhammad's commands and "Allah's promises" about the holy books were valid then, they are valid now.

- Invite the Muslim to read the Bible.

## "Strange, Miraculous Phenomena Attest to the Truth of Islam"

Muslims in just about every culture appeal to an unofficial though large body of anecdotal evidence for support of the truth of Islam. Such stories range from miracles that Muhammad and his successors allegedly performed to Neil Armstrong's hearing the call to prayer while on the moon (see discussion in chapter 2). I've been told that the Arabic numerals for "99" are written in the lines on the palm of the human hand (thus pointing every person to Allah's 99 beautiful names).

If you have the energy and resources to research each of these phenomena, you will probably find that the "evidence" is superficial, speculative, highly circumstantial, or just plain fabricated (as with the case of Neil Armstrong). However, a much simpler line of reasoning can be pursued.

*How authoritative are miracles for Islam?*

First, you should point out that Muhammad said that the truth of Islam was not to be established by miracles. In sura 3 of the Qur'an, Muhammad consoles his followers who are being criticized because he, their leader, had done no miracles, by saying that he had not done one because these wicked people would reject the sign if he gave one (see 3:183).[4] He says again in 6:37, "They say: 'Why is not a Sign sent down to him from his Lord?' Say: 'God hath certainly power to send down a sign. But most of them understand not.'" In both cases he makes clear that he would not do miracles as a way of attesting to the truth of his message. Wouldn't it be odd, then, for Allah to reverse his position and substantiate the truth of Islam today by miraculous signs?

---

Protestants have their own tales of angel sightings, miracles, and other strange phenomena.

---

Second, people of almost all religions have their own body of anecdotal evidence for supernatural phenomena. Medieval literature is replete with examples. The same is true today. A simple Internet search will reveal a massive number of stories and pictures about miraculous appearances of the Virgin Mary or Catholic saints. (In 2004 a grilled-cheese sandwich into which the Virgin had miraculously grilled an imprint of her face was sold on E-Bay for the price of $17,000.) Protestants have their own tales of angel sightings, miracles, and other strange phenomena. As David Hume observed, the fact that religions making contradictory truth claims both appeal to the miraculous invalidates the use of those miracles for proof.[5]

### Miracles of a different quality

You should then point out that the biblical appeal to the miraculous is of a fundamentally different nature than that of other religions. Biblical miracles, particularly the resurrection, are of such magnitude that their authenticity is more demonstrable. The New Testament appeals to two primary supernatural phenomena for support—fulfilled prophecy and the resurrection of Jesus.

Demonstrating to the Muslim the sheer number of prophecies fulfilled in the life of Jesus can be very convincing. It's been calculated that the chances of the Old Testament prophecies "coincidentally" being fulfilled in the life of Jesus are 1 in $10^{157}$. (1 in $10^{16}$ is the odds of covering the entire states of North

Carolina, South Carolina, and Virginia two feet deep in silver dollars and then picking out a single, predesignated one at random.)

The resurrection as a miracle stands in a class of its own. A number of works exist to demonstrate this, including Josh McDowell's *Evidence that Demands a Verdict* and Gary Habermas's *The Case for the Resurrection of Jesus*. The argument for the supernatural uniqueness of the resurrection goes like this:

1. No one doubts that the earliest Christians firmly believed Jesus had risen from the dead.

2. This is demonstrated by 1) the fact that the Lord's Supper, from the beginning, *celebrated* the death of Jesus in light of his resurrection; 2) the fact that baptism, from the beginning, has pictured Jesus' death and resurrection; 3) the fact that the early church worshipped on Sunday, the day of his resurrection; and 4) the apostles' frequent reference to the resurrection to validate their teaching (see 1 Corinthians 15:14; 1 John 1:1-4). Luke even summarizes the apostles' entire message as "the resurrection" (Acts 4:2). It is obvious that the early church's primary claim to the world was "Jesus has been resurrected."

3. This makes the likelihood that he had merely swooned on the cross impossible. A half-dead, badly weakened man could hardly have convinced his followers that he was the Prince of Life.

4. It is unlikely that the apostles deliberately lied about what they had seen, for they confessed even under torture and pain of martyrdom that they had seen him with their eyes. Although many people have died for false beliefs, it is implausible that the apostles died for something they *knew* to be false.

5. There is a clear problem with the idea the apostles somehow outwitted the Roman garrison guarding the tomb. And if the apostles were lying about Jesus' resurrection, Jesus' body would have been produced to disprove their claim.

6. It is also very unlikely that the appearances of Jesus were only hallucinations, due to the fact that so many saw him on numerous different occasions, and sometimes in large numbers at one time.

7. The crucifixion, resurrection, and vindication of the Messiah were predicted by many of the previous prophets (see Peter's sermon in Acts 2 and Isaiah 53:1-11).

*Talking points*

- Muhammad said that the truth of Islam was not to be established by miracles. It seems odd that Allah would reverse his position on the use of miracles. Thus, miraculous claims should not be used by Muslims to validate Islam.

- Almost all religions have similar anecdotal and apocryphal accounts of miracles, established by similar amounts of evidence. The fact that these miracles are used to support contradictory claims invalidates their use as proof.

- The two biblical appeals to the supernatural—fulfilled prophecy and the resurrection—are in a completely different category than other miracle claims, and the evidence supporting these claims approaches the level of overwhelming.

## "Christian Doctrines Are Complex and Hard to Understand, Which Proves Christianity Is Man-made. Islam's Simplicity Proves It Is from God."

The simplicity of the five pillars is one of the "secrets" to Islam's successes in the world. The essentials of Islam are easy to grasp and easily repeatable.

The simplicity of Islam also suggests to Muslims its truthfulness. Once I had a Muslim ask me whether a man on an island with no previous exposure to religion would be more likely to believe the Islamic or Christian explanation of God and salvation. Since a simple man could more easily grasp Islamic beliefs, my friend insisted, it proved that Islam was true.

*The obvious question*

Such a line of reasoning begs the question, however, assuming that simplicity is a proof of truthfulness. Neither the Qur'an nor the Bible says this anywhere. Furthermore, an uneducated man might find the explanation that the world is flat more compelling than that it is round. Theological truths, like scientific truths, are often beautiful in their complexity. If the study of the atom reveals nearly unfathomable wonder and mystery, how much more the study of the nature of God?

This question provides a good opportunity to explain the role of faith in revealed knowledge. Faith is accepting what you *cannot* understand based on what you *can* understand. It honors God when we trust what he says simply because we *know* it is he who is saying it. God has revealed some things we cannot easily understand, but he has given us ample evidence that it is he who is revealing them. As Moses explained, "The secret things belong to the LORD our God; but the things that are revealed belong to us and to our children forever" (Deuteronomy 29:29 RSV). Our role as believers is to ascertain whether or not the revelation is really from God. Once we know that it is, we must believe and obey regardless of how little it makes sense to us. As I've heard it said, "If my mind is the size of a soda can and God is the size of all the oceans, is it not silly to believe only the parts of him I can fit into my can?"

### Shifting the ground of discussion

To drive this point home, ask the Muslim, "If you were sure the Bible was from God, would you leave Islam and embrace Christ?" Ask him if he would suspend his intellectual problems with the Trinity if he knew the teaching were from God. If he says he would, then the question turns to "Has God given us sufficient proofs that it is he who has revealed himself in the Bible?" This puts the argument on a different plane—one on which the Christian can be much more persuasive. The biblical and evidential proofs for the identity and resurrection of Jesus are strong.

This simple question may also make the Muslim consider whether or not he prizes the acquisition of truth above everything else. Many Muslims (and Christians, for that matter) are simply followers of tradition rather than true seekers of God. Show him that to prioritize anything over knowing God is blasphemy. Jesus used this approach in John 7:17, when he said, "If any man's will is to do his will [that is, if anyone has predetermined to follow God's truth wherever it may lead], he shall know whether the teaching is from God or whether I am speaking on my own authority" (RSV). The decision to follow the revelation of God wherever it leads *precedes* the understanding that that revelation is true. Submission to truth is the *moral* dimension of faith, and it is as significant in approaching God as intellectual factors are.

## The story of Corinne

"Corinne" was a bright young Muslim college student from Turkey, studying journalism in the United States. Though attracted to Christianity, she had seemingly endless intellectual problems with the Trinity, salvation by grace alone, and other core Christian doctrines. When presented with the question of whether or not she would believe if she knew God had revealed it, she thought for a while and then said, "Now I see. I have made my own understanding a higher standard of truth than God's revelation. If he has revealed it, then I must believe it." She became increasingly convinced that the prophecies about Jesus, his claims, and the resurrection were true. Shortly thereafter she was visited by Jesus in a dream, and she became a follower of his the next morning.

### Talking points

- Simplicity is not the sole test for truthfulness in science, nor should it be in theology. For example, it may be easier to believe that the world is flat rather than round, but that does not make it so. If study of the atom reveals wonder and mystery, how much more study of the nature of God? Furthermore, neither the Bible nor the Qur'an says simplicity is a proof of truthfulness.

- Faith is accepting what you cannot understand based on what you can understand. The question of faith is, "If God has revealed it, will you believe it?" You can bring this to light for the Muslim by asking the simple question, "If God were to reveal to you the truths of Christianity in a way that you had no doubt in knowing they were really from him, would you follow them immediately, despite your 'intellectual problems' or the fact that it would alienate you from your society?" This question highlights the *moral* dimension of faith, which is as significant in conversion as the intellectual one (John 7:17). We must be committed to follow the truth regardless of where it leads.

## "God Cannot Be Known by Man"

Islamic theology states that God cannot be known. He is transcendent, beyond our ability to know. The Islamic doctrine of *tawhid* declares that there is an impassable gap between Creator and creation, and we can neither know God nor describe him by human language.

There is certainly some truth to this. We couldn't have a relationship with a transcendent God unless God revealed himself. We could not describe God unless he described himself, and even when he does there is a limitation in our language. Our descriptions of God point to his attributes but do not exhaust them.

But that said, the prophets claim that through them God has described himself and through that revelation he has invited us to know him (Isaiah 43:10-11; Micah 5:7; John 17:3). To say that God is unable to make himself known puts a limitation on God! So reframe this objection by asking, "Is God *able* to make himself known?"

You could also point out that saying God is unknowable is claiming to know something about God and is, in fact, attempting to describe him. You are assuming to have knowledge about the very thing you claim is unknowable, and describing the very thing you say is indescribable. Claiming that God is unknowable and indescribable is a self-defeating proposition.

### Talking points

- It is true that God could not be known by man unless God took it upon himself to reveal himself. The question should be, "Is God *able* to make himself known to man?" To say "no" is to put a limitation on him.

- The proposition that God cannot be known is self-defeating. Assuming that God is unknowable is assuming to know something about God.

10

# The Challenge
# and the Hope

Throughout our journey together in this book I have tried to offer you some "techniques" that will help you better understand and communicate with Muslims. However, as I said at the beginning, the awakening of Muslims to the gospel will not come as a result of any new technique we adopt. Seeing a Muslim come to Christ is a supernatural work of God. We can't engineer that. But God has promised to release his power in the lives of lost people in response to two things on our part: faith and sacrifice.

So, I want to close this book by reflecting with you on those two things.

## Intercessory Faith

*Faith* is understanding God's intentions for a situation and believing him for them. Faith is not something we just work up in our hearts; it is our trusting response to what God has indicated he wants to do.

*Intercession* means standing in someone else's place and representing them to God. Intercession is the role of a priest.

*Intercessory faith*, then, is standing in the place of a lost person and believing in what God wants to do in their lives, thereby releasing God's power on their behalf. Intercessory faith is the privilege and responsibility given to us as Christians, God's earthly "kingdom of priests" (1 Peter 2:9).

In Psalm 2:8, God the Father says to his Son, "Ask of Me, and I will give you the nations for your inheritance, and the ends of the earth for your possession." When we ask God, in Jesus' name, to help a lost person come to know Jesus, we are asking God to do what he has already promised Jesus he would do. Jesus told us to "go into all the world and preach the gospel" because "all authority" had been given to him. That authority is, in part, the authority to ask for "the lost nations" to come to him. As Psalm 2:8 says, he has "earned" them, and God promises to give them to him. Our role is to ask for them on his behalf. God has promised to give them to Jesus through our asking.

### The Matter of Unbelief

It is faith that unlocks the power for the mission of God. As I study the Bible, I become more and more convinced that what keeps God's power from pouring out on a particular people is not a lack of willingness or ability on God's part, but unbelief on the part of the church! God's intentions have been made clear. It is our unbelief that restrains him.

Isaiah said that God's arm is not shortened so that it cannot save (in other words, God's power is fully sufficient to open even the most hardened Muslim heart), and his ear is not heavy that he cannot hear (God is overflowing with compassion, sufficient to save even the most resistant of Muslims). In other words, it is not a deficiency in God's power or mercy that keeps the Muslim world from coming to Christ. It is a deficiency of something in us. We don't yet believe God enough to release his power among them.

> Intercessors stand in the unbelieving gap
> between God and the object of his love and
> believe in his power and willingness to save.

Matthew 13:58 says of Nazareth that Jesus "did not do many mighty works there because of their *unbelief.*" It was not that Jesus was unwilling or unable. It's just that there was no one there to believe him and release his power. All it took was a believing touch of the hem of his garment, and a flood of power was released.

When Jesus performed the miracle of the feeding of the 5000, Scripture says it was a "test" for the disciples (John 6:6). What was he testing? He was testing whether or not they would know what to do, after he had gone, when they were faced with a starving multitude and not nearly enough resources. What Jesus taught them in that miracle was that everything that is necessary for the feeding of the multitude is already in the hands of the church! We simply must believe what he can do with it and offer what we have to him, and we will see that there is more than enough in his hands to get the job done.

That means that our primary role with Muslims is to believe God on their behalf. Intercessors are not simply people who pray on behalf of others, as if God needed us to inform him about how lost Muslims are. No, intercessors *believe* on behalf of others. Intercessors stand in the unbelieving gap between God and the object of his love and believe in his power and willingness to save.

In other words, the reason God's power has not been released in the Muslim world is, in large part, because there have not been intercessors in their midst, believing on their behalf, allowing Jesus to multiply the bread of life to the salvation of their souls.

*Would you let that sink in for a minute?* What now separates people from salvation is not God's unwillingness, but our unbelief.

## Will God Not Act If We Ask?

Is it not time to believe Jesus' promise on behalf of the Muslim world? Is it not time, in the words of William Carey, to "expect great things *from* God, and attempt great things *for* God"? Currently, only 6 percent of the Western Christian mission force is working for the salvation of Muslims. How much regret will we feel when we realize that God would have worked through us for them had we only believed his promise and interceded on their behalf?

Hudson Taylor said concerning his pioneering work in China,

> We have to do with One who is Lord of all power and might, whose arm is not shortened that it cannot save, nor His ear heavy that it cannot hear; with One whose unchanging Word directs us to ask and receive that our joy may be full, to open our mouths wide, that He may fill them. And we do well to remember that this gracious God, who has condescended to place His almighty power at the command of believing prayer looks not lightly on the bloodguiltiness of those who neglect to avail themselves of it for the benefit of the perishing...
>
> I had no doubt but that if I prayed for fellow-workers, in the name of the Lord Jesus Christ, they would be given. I had no doubt but that, in answer to such prayer, the means for our going forth

would be provided, and that doors would be opened before us
in unreached parts of the Empire…The sense of bloodguiltiness
became more and more intense. Simply because I refused to ask
for them, the laborers did not come forward, did not go out to
China: and every day tens of thousands in that land were passing
into Christless graves![1]

Today, there are estimates that as many as 30,000 people a day are being
baptized in China due to the faith of Hudson Taylor and many other believing Christians, both Chinese and international.[2] *Is it not time to believe God
on behalf of the Muslims?* Isn't God as ready and willing to save as he ever has
been? Will he not do it for Muslims as he has done it for others?

Recently I was visiting some Christian friends in a Muslim country. I
stood on the shore where a tsunami wave had come through just a few years
before and killed over 150,000 people. As I stood there, I got angry. *"Why,
God?"* I asked. "Why did you send a wave of destruction when you could
have sent a wave of salvation?"

I don't know why. But in that moment God's Spirit reminded me that
is why he has my Christian friends there…they are there *to believe God* on
behalf of the Muslims, and by believing to release that wave of his mercy.

I am ready for God's wave of salvation to come to Muslims, and I am
working expectantly. As I said in the introduction, I plan to be like the
woodpecker pecking away at the telephone pole when lightning strikes the
pole and splits it in two. When it happens, I'm sure I will be a little startled,
but not surprised. I always knew it would come. God said it would.

That is why *you* are there in the life of your Muslim friend. You are
there to believe on his or her behalf, and by believing to release the power
of God's work in their life. So ask boldly, in his name, and don't be surprised when he answers.

## Sacrifice

There is one other indispensable element Jesus said was necessary for
salvation to come to the world.

*Our death.*

In John 12, Jesus was approached by a group of Greeks who wanted to
learn about him. They told Philip, "Sir, we wish to see Jesus" (verse 21). This
was a significant moment in Jesus' life. It had been clear from the beginning that Jesus' purpose was to come not just for the Jews, but for the whole

world—for "the Greeks" (who here represent the entire non-Jewish world) now standing before him. In light of that, Jesus' response is startling.

Instead of turning to the Greeks, he says something *to his disciples.* He tells them that a harvest of salvation will only come to these Greeks if they will plant themselves, like seeds in the ground, and die. The life of "the Greeks" would only come through the death of the disciples.

The "life" of Muslims will only come through the "death" of the church.

## More Remains to Be Done

Paul said that we must "fill up in our bodies what is lacking in the wounds of Christ." What could be "lacking" in the wounds of Christ? Didn't Jesus *finish* the work of salvation? In one sense, yes. However, in another, the work of the cross is not finished. The news of the cross has to be shared with others to be of any real value to them.

That's where we come in. The gospel will go forward in Muslims only through our wounds. Wounds are not simply an unfortunate byproduct of our witness to Muslims, but the means by which they will hear and believe.

If suffering were only an occasional consequence of preaching the gospel, we might be able to figure out how to avoid suffering, sacrifice, and death and still accomplish our mission. But we cannot. For the gospel to really live in Muslims, we will have to pour out our lives for them as Jesus poured his out for us.

We will have to choose to befriend Muslims on our campus or in our community even when it would be more comfortable to spend time with people like ourselves. We will have to choose to devote time to praying for them. We will have to endure, gracefully, their misunderstanding and reproach. We will have to give our money with radical generosity to support ministry to Muslims around the world. Many of us will have to leave a comfortable life and go to live in a foreign culture very far from our families. Many of us will have to be willing to let our children grow up and do the same.

When the gospel begins to flourish among Muslims, persecution will come. Some believers will suffer and die. It's always been that way.

## My Own Experience

I have never felt the full terror of Muslim persecution, but I have felt some of its tremors. My experiences are not even worthy of being compared to the terrible price that some missionaries to Muslims have paid, but I know firsthand that success in these "unreached" places will come only at great personal cost!

While serving among a Muslim unreached people group, my team attempted to distribute a newly translated New Testament, both in written and audio form. This would have been the first copy of the Bible our people group would ever have seen in their native tongue. To accomplish the task, we brought in four volunteers. I met with these volunteers, delivered the Bibles to them, and helped them plot their 21-day journey.

---

"Not ashamed" means "not unwilling" to pay the ultimate sacrifice for the spread of the gospel.

---

On day four, a mob of close to 2500 people converged on them. The police "rescued" them from the mob and put them in prison. The mob demanded that the police release these four men so they could kill them. The police refused, and a minor gun battle ensued. The police prevailed, and in protest, the mob burned the cars of both my friends and the chief of police.

My friends did not speak the local language, and the police did not speak English. The process was stymied, they told me, until a policeman emerged who greeted them in English. He said, "I am the only man here who speaks English. I have been informed about what you were doing, and I must tell you that I am honored to meet you. I am a new Christian, having been one now for less than a year. I was transferred up to this area, against my will, about four months ago. I will do whatever I can to help you."

This policeman contacted the U.S. embassy, which sent a helicopter to extract the men. When the helicopter arrived, however, the people in the crowd that was now camped out in front of the police station started shooting at it, and the helicopter had to withdraw. At this point, the Christian policeman hid the men in the back of a truck, smuggled them out of the area, and had them flown out of the country.

In the process of these events, detectives from the national government came down to investigate the situation. A link was quickly established between the imprisoned men and my team, and the government people came for us. My neighbor, a "governor" of considerable influence in the region, flatly refused to turn over any of our team members to them, saying he took personal responsibility for our actions. The mayor placed me under a type of house arrest (for my safety) until the uproar had subsided.

The one thing I remember most clearly about this whole situation is how terrified I was. I did not react with the bravery I always imagined I would. It is one thing to say you'd give your life for Christ; it is quite another to think someone is about to take you up on that offer. Throughout those fearful days I pleaded with God for some type of promise that he would keep me safe. But he never gave me any promise like that. What he did remind me of was that my salvation had come through Christ's death, and that the salvation of Muslims would come through ours. I knew God was asking me to make one simple determination: *Was the spread of the gospel worth more to me than my life?*

It was during this time that I think I first understood what Paul meant in Romans 1:16 when he said, "I am not ashamed of the gospel of Christ, for it is the power of God to salvation for the Jew first but also for the Greek." "Not being ashamed of the gospel" was Paul's somber declaration that he believed the gospel coming to the Romans was worth more to him than his life. "Not ashamed" means "not unwilling" to pay the ultimate sacrifice for the spread of the gospel.

Eventually, the fervor subsided in our region and the investigation was dropped...though I'm still not sure why. There was more than enough evidence to implicate our team and the nationals working with us. My neighbor, who had stepped in to protect me, knew I had copies of the exact same "book" the team was passing out. My only explanation is that God must have confounded the investigators and kept the door open for our team to continue to work in peace.

The New Testaments and gospel recordings the team gave out became famous in the region. The Islamic police had set about to recover all the copies handed out, but they were able to track down only a few of them. Today, the work of Christians in this people group continues and is now thriving under the lead of a strong team of national believers.

God brings the harvest through the sacrifices of the church.

## How Are You Called?

Perhaps you don't live in a place where you'll face this type of danger. But if you've made it this far in this book, I suspect God is calling you, in some way, to be a part of bringing Muslims to Christ. Sacrifices happen on all levels, large and small. Why not begin by committing to pray daily for the salvation of Muslims? Or, reach across the cultural divide in your own city or on your own campus and befriend a Muslim. Perhaps you could begin to give generously to support the work among Muslims in the world. Talk to your pastor about your church engaging an unreached Muslim community in the world. Or maybe you should consider going yourself to live in a Muslim country. Or ask God to send your children.

The point I am trying to make is that if we are really serious about seeing Muslims comes to Christ, we must be willing to pay the price. Reaching Muslims cost Jesus his life. If we are to reach Muslims, it will cost us ours as well.

Let me conclude this book by sharing a story that has long inspired me. The biography of Adoniram Judson was the first book placed in my hands after I became a Christian. Judson's story was what God used to open my eyes to the condition of our world and God's intentions for it. His story exemplifies the price that must be paid for the gospel to flourish in an unreached land.

---

Adoniram Judson was a seed that
fell into the ground and died.

---

Judson was 24 years old when he went to the "impossible" country of Burma (now Myanmar). He worked there for 38 years until his death at age 61. When he entered Burma in 1813, it would have been "closed" by today's standards—it had a brutally despotic emperor and little religious toleration, and was at war with neighboring countries. Even William Carey advised Judson not to go to there.[3]

The price Judson paid was immense. His first wife, Ann, who left for Burma with him, bore three children, all of whom died. The first baby, nameless, was born dead just as they sailed from India to Burma. The second child, Roger Williams Judson, lived 17 months and then died. The third, Maria Elizabeth Butterworth Judson, lived to be two and died. Ann died six months later.[4] Judson spent the last period of Ann's life being tortured in a Burmese prison—able neither to spend time with her nor to continue his mission work. Ultimately, his time in Burma would cost him the loss of seven children, numerous colleagues, and almost perpetual painful bodily maladies.

Judson would not consider leaving, however. He said, "Life is short.

Millions of Burmese are perishing. I am almost the only person on earth who has attained their language to communicate salvation."[5]

Operation World now estimates the Myanmar Baptist Convention to be 3700 congregations with 617,781 members and 1,900,000 affiliates.[6] David Barrett says in the *World Christian Encyclopedia* that the establishment of Christianity in Burma owes itself to the pioneering work of a single man.[7] Adoniram Judson was a seed that fell into the ground and died. The "Burma story" came to life through Judson's death.

The life of Adoniram Judson inspires me because the Muslim story has, for the most part, yet to be written. As I put down these final words, I am once again deep in the heart of a Muslim country. Being here again reminds me of how often I have despaired of whether this great work will ever be done. Will we ever see a mass movement of Muslims erupting in praise to God our Savior? The task seems impossible! For many it is not that they have not heard, but that they do not want to hear! But God has said that his fame will one day cover the earth "as the waters cover the sea." One day, his salvation will be known and cherished by a vast number of Muslims that no one can number. Nothing is too hard for God!

I am certain of two things regarding Muslims turning to Christ: 1) *It will happen*; and 2) *it will happen through our faith and our blood.* Perhaps mine. Perhaps my children's.

I want to believe God on behalf of his promise about Muslims, and I want to follow Jesus in reaching them, wherever he leads. Will you join me?

It is time for the church to ask God for the nations he promised to Jesus as his inheritance. It is time to ask God to bless us, the church, so that we can bless the Muslim world with the gospel (Psalm 67:2). So I pray, with Judson,

> *O God, have mercy on the churches in the United States…continue and perpetuate the heavenly revivals of religion which they have begun to enjoy; and may the time soon come when no church shall dare to sit under Sabbath and sanctuary privileges without having one of their number to represent them on heathen ground.*
>
> *Have mercy on the theological seminaries, and hasten the time when*

*one half of all who yearly enter the ministry shall be taken by thine Holy Spirit, and driven into the wilderness, feeling a sweet necessity laid on them, and the precious love of Christ and of souls constraining them.*

*Hear, O Lord, all the prayers which are this day presented in all the monthly concerts throughout the habitable globe, and hasten the millennial glory, for which we are all longing, and praying, and laboring… Come, O our Bridegroom; come, Lord Jesus!*

Let's believe, hope, and labor together. I am praying for you.

# Additional Resources

## Muslim Life, Culture, and Practice

Braswell, George W., Jr., *Islam: Its Prophet, Peoples, Politics, and Power.* Nashville, TN: Broadman and Holman Publishers, 1996. A very good overview of Islam from a Christian theologian who lived in Iran and has studied Islam for a lifetime.

Nasr, Seyyed Hossein. *The Heart of Islam: Enduring Values for Humanity.* San Francisco: HarperCollins, 2002. A great, moderate treatment of contemporary Islam written by one of Islam's primary modern spokesmen. Nasr is an excellent, clear writer.

———. *Islam: Religion, History and Civilization.* New York: HarperOne, 1991.

## English Translations of the Qur'an and Hadith

*The Glorious Qur'an*, translation and commentary by Abdullah Yusuf Ali. This is one of the standard English translations.

Guillaume, Alfred. *The Traditions of Islam.* Salem, NH: Ayer Company Publishers, Inc., 1987.

www.iiu.edu.my/deed/hadith/. This site contains an extensive collection of the major Hadith traditions, organized by topic.

## Apologetics and Christian Response

Ankerberg, John, and Emir Caner. *The Truth About Islam and Jihad.* Eugene, OR: Harvest House Publishers, 2009. A short, helpful resource giving you an overview of key texts and modern interpretations of *jihad*.

Caner, Emir Fethi, and Ergun Mehmet Caner. *More than a Prophet: An Insider's Response to Muslim Beliefs About Jesus and Christianity.* Grand Rapids, MI: Kregel Publications, 2003.

———. *Unveiling Islam: An Insider's Look at Muslim Life and Beliefs.* Grand Rapids, MI: Kregel Publications, 2002. The Caners are converts to Christianity from a Turkish Muslim family. Both are well-spoken, and they are able to give a stirring, firsthand depiction of Islam from the inside. They are not gentle in their treatment of the religion, but they are very convincing.

Geisler, Norman, and Abdul Saleeb. *Answering Islam*, 2nd ed. Grand Rapids, MI: Baker, 2002. A definitive work on the historical, logical, and factual shortcomings of Islam. A must-have reference.

George, Timothy. *Is the God of Muhammad the Father of Jesus?* Grand Rapids, MI: Zondervan, 2002. A well-balanced work by one of Christianity's finest scholars. George's expertise is not in Islam, but this is a good, thorough book nonetheless.

Muller, Roland. *The Messenger, the Message, the Community: Three Critical Issues for the Cross-Cultural Church Planter.* WEC Publications, 2006.

Musk, Bill A. *Touching the Soul of Islam: Sharing the Gospel in Muslim Cultures.* Crowborough, U.K.: Broadway House, 1995. This book will take you deep into Muslim superstition. If you are intrigued by how Muslims "fill in the gap" left by the Islamic doctrine of God's transcendence with a vast system of intermediaries, this book will fascinate you.

Orris, Lorraine. *Islam 101: Reaching Out with Understanding.* Peachtree City, GA: New Life Publications, 2004. A great one-stop introduction to Islam for people who want to befriend Muslims.

Parshall, Phil. *Bridges to Islam: A Christian Perspective on Folk Islam.* Grand Rapids, MI: Baker Book House, 1983. Parshall has spent a lifetime studying Islam. This is a great short summary of some of his best work.

Warraq, Ibn. *Why I Am Not a Muslim.* Amherst, NY: Prometheus Books, 1995. Warraq is an insider who speaks about the abuses of fundamentalist Islam and the difficulty of living under a Muslim regime.

www.AlwaysBeReady.com. The Web site of Charlie H. Campbell, the director of Always Be Ready Apologetics Ministry, which includes several helpful print and multimedia resources on Islam.

www.Answering-Islam.org. This Web site offers strong biblical and historical responses to Islamic theology and culture.

www.ApologeticsIndex.org. An extensive apologetics database including substantial engagement in Islamic history, beliefs, and practices.

## The Lives of Muslim Women

Adeney, Miriam. *Daughters of Islam*. Downers Grove, IL: InterVarsity Press, 2002.

Ankerberg, John, and Emir Caner. *The Truth About Islam and Women*. Eugene, OR: Harvest House Publishers, 2009.

Caner, Ergun Mehmet. *Voices Behind the Veil: The World of Islam Through the Eyes of Women*. Grand Rapids, MI: Kregel Publications, 2003.

Cate, Mary Ann, and Karol Downey. *From Fear to Faith: Muslim and Christian Women*. Pasadena, CA: William Carey Library, 2003.

Eckhart, Jeleta, and Fran Love. *Ministry to Muslim Women: Longing to Call Them Sisters*. Pasadena, CA: William Carey Publishers, 2003.

Hosseini, Khaled. *A Thousand Splendid Suns*. New York: Riverhead Books, 2007. This book and its predecessor, *The Kite Runner*, are two of the most stirring novels I have ever read. They are set in Afghanistan. *A Thousand Splendid Suns* is about the life of two Muslim women, and the *Kite Runner* is about two Muslim boys.

Lamb, Christina. *The Sewing Circles of Herat*. New York: HarperCollins Publishers, 2002.

Mallouhi, Christine. *Miniskirts, Mothers, and Muslims*. Grand Rapids, MI: Kregel Publications, 2004.

## The Lives of Muslim Men

Hamid, Mohsin. *The Reluctant Fundamentalist*. Orlando, FL: Harcourt, Inc., 2007. Fascinating.

Hosseini, Khaled. *The Kite Runner*. New York: Riverhead Books, 2003. *The Kite Runner* is about two young Afghan boys and their life through the wars, the time of Taliban rule, and the rebuilding of Afghanistan. It will tear at your heart!

## Islam and World Affairs

Huntington, Samuel. *The Clash of Civilizations and the Remaking of World Order.* London: Free Press, 2002. A classic book describing why Islam has come into such conflict with the West and the coming crisis between the nations of "Muhammad and Paul."

Lewis, Bernard. *The Crisis of Islam: Holy Way and Unholy Terror.* New York: The Modern Library, 2003. Lewis is the preeminent Western scholar on Islam. He has written extensively, and this is one of his best, most concise works. He always writes with great insight.

Appendix

# Speaking in Islamic Code:

## *How Far Is Too Far?*

Islam, because of its similarities to Christianity, provides some great places to begin conversation with Muslims about the gospel. Islam has given Muslims a glimpse of the majesty of God. It has taught them to be "submitted" to him. (Remember, the very name "Muslim" means "one submitted to God.") The Muslim moral code is very similar to the Christian one. Islam brought Arab peoples far down the path toward Christianity, teaching them to abandon idolotry and fear the one, true God.

For this reason, some missionaries to Muslims consider Islam to be a divinely appointed "halfway house" on the road to Christ. Some even call Muslim converts to Christianity "completed Muslims," much like Jewish converts to Jesus were considered "completed Jews." They consider Muhammad a prophet in that, like Moses, he taught his people to worship the one true God.

Can you refer to Muhammed, then, as a "prophet," and the Qur'an as a "prophetic book"? Can Muslims who embrace the Lordship of Jesus still pray in a mosque with other Muslims, only now in the name of Jesus? Can they continue to call themselves "Muslims," only now knowing that true submission to God is found in submission to Jesus? Can the name *Allah*, which literally means "the deity," be used for God, rather than God's Hebrew name, *Yahweh* or its Latin counterpart, *Jehovah*? Can Jesus be referred to by his Qur'anic name, *Isa al-Masih*? Can communities of believers worship in the forms and customs of the mosque (that is, on Fridays, using ritual prayers, with shoes off, separated by gender, and so on)?

## The Contextualization Question

How "Muslim" can the gospel look? Theologians refer to this as "the contextualization question." It is a difficult one. On the one hand, we know that some of Paul's strongest words in the New Testament were for people who could not take the gospel out of Jewish culture. Paul insisted that Gentile converts did not need to adopt Hebrew language and customs when they became Christians. Surely Muslims do not need to adopt Western ways of talking and dressing or styles of expression when they become Christians.

> How "Muslim" can we make
> Christianity without corrupting it?

But on the other, we know that God demands we worship him in his way. The second command insists that we not pollute God's gospel with any mixture of man-originated worship. So, when it comes to Islamic terms and practices, what can we use? How "Muslim" can we make Christianity without corrupting it?

This was one of the most difficult questions I faced when I first arrived in a Muslim country. A well-meaning believer had told me I could pray, as a believer in Jesus, in a mosque during an Islamic prayer service. After all, Muslims are praying to the "one, true God," and there is nothing sacred about a church building. God can just as easily be worshipped in a building with an onion-top dome as he can in one with a steeple. I would not pray, of course, with Qur'anic verses; I would pray through the name of Jesus. It made sense to me, so I tried it. I was super nervous, but a Muslim friend promised to guide me through it.

### Bad contextualization almost got me killed!

I went through the washing with my friend, "symbolically" demonstrating my need for cleanness before God. I took my role in the line of Muslim men bowing for prayer. Somehow I got shoved into the very front row of the prayer lines...as if the presence of a large white guy was not awkward enough, there I was on the front row. I recited "There is no God but God" at the appropriate time, as I believed that. I mumbled, "Jesus Christ is his Son" when everyone else said, "And Muhammad is his prophet." I waved my hands by my ears and brought them down to my belly showing that we listen to God's word and take it into our hearts. I bowed with my head on the floor at the appropriate time showing my reverence before God. I sat up on my ankles (a peculiarly uncomfortable posture for an awkward white guy) and recited verses.

I noticed that everyone else had their right hand resting on their hip with their index finger pointed and thumb cocked, so I did that. I asked my friend what this meant, and he whispered that the one finger indicated that there was only one God (I was okay with that) and the cocked thumb meant that Muhammad was his prophet (so I quietly straightened out my thumb).

I managed to finish the prayer ritual in one piece and without major incident—other than the fact that I accidentally, instinctively sung the harmony when they did the collective *amen* at the end...evidently Southern gospel music hasn't swept Islam yet. Actually...funny story...when I did that, it made me really start to laugh, uncontrollably, realizing how out of place it had been. Thankfully, we had all gone down with heads to the floor for our final prayer bow, so no one could see my chest heaving with laughter. I knew that if the white guy were caught guffawing during prayer the experience could end very badly, so while we were doing the final obeisance, I prayed earnestly, "Please God, help me stop laughing. Please. These people will kill me if they think I'm making fun." Thankfully, God heard my prayer.

Was I right in trying to pray in Jesus' name in the mosque? Is it okay for Christians to express truth in Muslim language, and to try to "redeem" Muslim worship expressions? Is it okay to follow Jesus *within* Islam, and not leave it?

In this appendix I will attempt to answer that question. First, let me summarize the various ways that evangelical missionaries have attempted to answer it, and then offer a theological analysis and hopefully some helpful guidelines.

The nature of this appendix requires that the language I use be a little more theologically technical than the rest of the book, but if you stick with it, I think you'll find working through this to be a rewarding exercise.

## "C-1" to "C-6"

How much Muslim-background-believers should incorporate Islamic culture (language, styles, traditions, and so on) into their Christian worship is usually rated on the "C-1 to C-6 spectrum," developed by long-term missionary to Muslims John Travis.[1] Here's how it breaks down, starting with the least contextualized:[2]

*C-1: Traditional church using outsider language.*[3] These are churches that are found within Muslim cultures but use the languages, traditions, and even building structures of the Christian culture from which they come. There are thousands of such churches in Muslim countries—some of which pre-date Islamization. Some of them are thriving.

*C-2: Traditional church using insider language.* This approach is very similar to C1, except that Christians in these churches have adopted the local language. They still use "non-Muslim" names for God, Jesus, and the Scriptures (often deriving from Latin or English roots). Believers are called "Christians," even if the term has more ethnic or political significance than it does religious.

*C-3: Contextualized Christ-centered communities using insider language and religiously neutral insider cultural forms.* Christians in these churches adopt the dress, language, and customs of the local Muslim culture. They avoid using distinctly Islamic religious customs, like prayer postures or worship styles. Sometimes these congregations meet in traditional church buildings, sometimes in more neutral locations. C-3 believers call themselves "Christians."

*C-4: Contextualized Christ-centered communities using insider language and biblically permissible cultural and Islamic forms.* In this approach, not only are neutral cultural forms absorbed from the surrounding culture, but also biblically permissible Islamic religious customs (like praying prostrate, removing shoes when entering a sanctuary, refraining from pork, praying with raised hands, and so on). Arabic/Islamic terms are used for God (*Allah*), Jesus (*Isa al-Masih*), and the Scriptures (*al-Kitab*). These believers do not meet in traditional church buildings. Believers call themselves "followers of Jesus" or some other alternative to "Christians." Muslims still see these believers as non-Muslims, however. C-4 Christians often distance themselves from C-1 and C-2 believers, so as not to create unnecessary cultural obstacles for Muslims who are interested in Christianity.

*C-5: Christ-centered communities of "Messianic Muslims" who have acknowledged Jesus as Lord and Savior.* In the C-5 approach, followers of Jesus retain their identity as Muslims. They consider themselves similar to "Messianic Jews," in that they see the "Old Covenant" of Islam now fulfilled in Christ. They often call themselves "Completed Muslims" or "Muslims who follow Isa al-Masih." Those parts of Islamic theology that are deemed incompatible with the Bible are reinterpreted or quietly discarded. C-5 believers are usually aggressive in trying to convert their Muslim neighbors to Jesus. Often, they come to be seen by other Muslims as theologically deviant, and may eventually be kicked out of Islamic society. Many C-5 Christians have no problem continuing to worship at the mosque, seeing it as a "neutral" place of worship and prayer to the one true God.[4]

*C-6: Small Christ-centered communities of secret/underground believers.* In those cases where isolated Muslims come to faith within a harsh, repressive community, some believers choose to retain their identity as Muslims and worship Christ secretly. Often these believers come to Christ through a direct revelation (dream), through reading a Bible, or through hearing a gospel broadcast. Because they know no other believers, they have no fellowship. They continue to call themselves Muslims and are viewed as Muslims by everyone around them. They are only secretly Christians. (To note, no prominent missiologists consider this to be a healthy, permanent state.)

## The Theological Basis for Contextualization

Is there a biblical basis for contextualization? Definitely. Our Bible is itself proof of that! God communicated to us in a language that we could understand. Furthermore, God came to us, in our flesh—as a man we could understand, identify with, and touch.

Proper contextualization is expressing the truth in a way that that culture can understand it, *not* changing the truth so a culture will accept it. Proper contextualization distinguishes between those behaviors and customs which are a necessary response to the holiness of God (like telling the truth), and those which are simply one culture's way of expressing a particular truth (such as bowing your head as a sign of reverence before God).

The apostle Paul was zealous to separate the truth of the gospel from cultural tradition. He insisted that the gospel was not bound to the Jewish language, culture, or ethnic identity. If there were *ever* a culture that could argue that it was God-prescribed, it would be Judaism! God used Hebrew words to teach divine concepts. God gave Jewish customs, holidays, and traditions as cultural manifestations of divine truth.

Yet, Paul insisted, Hebrew culture, language, styles and modes of worship, holidays, and religious symbols were not essential to the gospel, and thus did not need to be part of the gospel "package." The living water of the gospel, Paul insisted, must be extracted from its cultural "cup" and placed within the cup of the culture it is seeking to penetrate. For Paul, that meant becoming "all things to all men." In many aspects of culture, Paul would not require his hearers to become like him, he would become like *them*! When with Jews he observed the Jewish laws, holidays, and customs, and with Gentiles he would discard those things. He was well-versed in whatever culture he was trying to reach, and drew from their unique historical and philosophical traditions in teaching them the gospel.

This, of course, does not mean that all aspects of culture are adaptable to the gospel. As 1 John says, the world is an "enemy" to God. When the Christian message absorbs "worldly" patterns of thinking, the gospel is lost. Rather than the gospel confronting and redeeming the culture, culture has corrupted and obscured the gospel. Theologians call this *syncretization*.

## Removing Hindrances

However, proper contextualization removes many of the stumbling blocks a culture has with the gospel. It tries to make the gospel less "foreign." All cultures place value on their unique traditions and customs. "Foreigners" are looked upon with distrust, for they threaten to undo the unifying fabric of society! When the cultural foreignness of the gospel is removed, hearers are enabled to consider the true heart of the gospel: repentance toward God, faith in his Messiah, and genuine worship in spirit and truth.

Rejecting one's culture is not only *unnecessary*, according to the gospel, it is *undesirable* as well. Converting out of one's culture goes against God's creative order and redemptive plan for creation. God was the one who created the rich diversity of cultures. He was the one who appointed men to live in different ethnic groups.[5] The Son of God's final "congregation" will include people of "every tribe, tongue and nation" under heaven (Revelation 7:9), who will bring "the wealth of the nations" into heaven (Revelation 21:26).

For Muslims this problem of foreignness is magnified because of their sordid past with Christian civilizations. The word *Christian* conjures up images of colonialization, the Crusades, capitalistic exploitation, cultural arrogance, and American pop culture. I was once told by a teenage Muslim girl that she wanted our family to throw her a "Christian" party for her birthday, because her "Muslim" parties were boring. By that she meant a party with dancing, skimpy clothing, and beer, because this is what she saw cross-wearing MTV stars doing! For the Muslim, becoming a "Christian" implies rejecting a lot of customs that seem righteous and good and embracing things they believe to be (and truly are) sinful!

## The Gospel's Adaptability

Proper contextualization has been a key to successful Christian mission in the past. Rodney Stark points out in *The Rise of Christianity* that one of the key factors in the rapid spread of the gospel through the Roman Empire was its ability to adapt to any culture. There were thousands of religions in ancient Rome, but each was tied to a particular people group and corresponding heritage and customs. Worshipping a new god meant also adopting the cultural forms associated with that god. Christians were one of the only groups in the Roman Empire that not only recognized the legitimacy of cultural diversity, but celebrated it. Their culturally mixed congregations stood in stark contrast to the culturally divided temples of the pagans! Believers of various cultures had a bond in the gospel that transcended their cultures.

Some of the most successful missionaries in the past 200 years have been aggressive with contextualization. Hudson Taylor and Lottie Moon both donned traditional Chinese dress and customs in their work with the Chinese. Philip Jenkins has noted that the rapid spread of the gospel among the Latin American and African countries is due, in part, to the "Latinization" and "Africanization" of the gospel.[6]

## The Case for C-5 and C-6

Advocates of the C-5 approach believe that contextualization means presenting Islam as the prophetic forerunner of the gospel and Jesus as the fulfillment of the Qur'an. They want to see movements to Jesus *within* Islam rather than *from* Islam. These are called *insider movements*.

Advocates of the C-5 approach see insider movements in both the Old and New Testaments. The people of Nineveh who repented at the preaching of Jonah did not become Jews, they say, but became Ninevite worshippers of God.

After Naaman acknowledged Jehovah as the only true God (2 Kings 5:15), he asked Elisha in advance for forgiveness for when he would bow down at the "temple of Rimmon" (verse 18). Elisha granted the forgiveness, knowing, C-5 proponents claim, that Naaman really would be bowing in his heart to Jehovah, the only actual God, even as he bowed his knees before Rimmon.

---

"Allah has 100 names. Man knows 99 of these names,
but only the camel knows the one-hundredth name."

---

In John 4, Jesus told the Samaritan woman that a time was coming when what would matter about worship was not where it was done, but only that it was "in spirit and in truth." After this conversation, when she and many other Samaritans believed in Jesus, there is no indication they ceased worshipping God at Gerizim or that Jesus quit worshipping in the Jerusalem temple.[7] The issue was not the forms of Jewish or Samaritan worship but that they worshipped the one true God in spirit and truth. In the same manner, C-5 advocates say, Jesus points Muslims beyond their religious forms to worship the one true God *properly*. Muslims, having found God in spirit and truth through the Messiah, may continue to worship under the rubric of Islam, now seeing Jesus as the fulfillment of the Islamic quest for God.

Kevin Greeson's "Camel" method,[8] a popular tool among C-5 advocates, argues that the Qur'an should be used as a "gospel tract" pointing Muslims to Jesus. Jesus is the "missing element" of the Qur'an, and the Qur'an (properly read) points to him. The name of the method, "Camel," comes from an old Arab proverb: "Allah has 100 names. Man knows 99 of these names, but only the camel knows the one-hundredth name." Muslims are urged to learn "the secret of the camel," which is that the one-hundredth name of Allah is Isa al-Masih (Jesus Christ).

Some proponents of C-5 believe that C-6 and C-5 are necessary stages in the conversion of an Islamic community. They believe that a movement toward the gospel may start C-5 and C-6 and move toward C-4 or C-3. Others think a believing community can remain perpetually a C-5, as God delights in the diversity of and his varied work in the nations.

## Problems with the C-5 and C-6 Approaches

### *Theological Problems*

There is certainly much to learn from those advocating the C-5 approach. However, the case for C-5 rests largely on a false premise: that because both Judaism and Islam play a "preparatory" role to Christian faith, Islam's role in the Muslim-Christian convert's life will be the same as Judaism's role in many Jewish-Christian converts' lives.

This premise misses the crucial distinction between *special* and *general* revelation. The Jewish Old Testament was the verbally inspired Word of God, not simply the "best" of the pre-Christian religions. Jesus acknowledged *every* word of the Hebrew Scriptures to be true. If a Jewish prophet was not accurate in all he said, he was to be stoned! In other words, Muhammad cannot be compared to a Jewish prophet. He may have gotten a few things right, but he did not speak with divine authority.

Still, couldn't Islam be recognized as a divinely given, "prophetic" (even if imperfect) precursor of Christ? And if so, can we not acknowledge Muhammad as a "prophet" in that sense?

The answer is no. The Old Testament prophets preached about God's salvation, by grace, through faith. Old Testament prophets did not simply "prepare" the Jewish people for the gospel, *they preached the gospel themselves*. Israel was a *covenant* community, not simply a "prepared" people. Muhammad did not preach salvation by grace through faith. He preached works-righteousness, which is the enemy of the gospel. Islamic communities never have been, and never will be, covenant communities.

***There is only one gospel.*** Some Christian traditions mistakenly have taught that men pre-Christ were saved in a way other than by faith in God's redemptive work—by the keeping of the Law, obedience to conscience, and so on. In this sense, some assume that just as Moses "prepared" the Jews to receive the "new gospel" or "new Covenant," so Muhammad prepared the Muslim peoples to receive their new covenant.

But this is to terribly misunderstand the Old Testament. The apostle Paul explains that the gospel of Jesus is nothing fundamentally new to Jewish religion. David, Abraham, and Moses all preached the same gospel that Paul preached—justification by faith in God's promise (Romans 1:17; 4:7-8; 4:12; Galatians 3:5-12). The Jewish religion and customs were to be Christ's perfect shadow, an infallible imprint of the gospel. The second commandment of the Law had made clear that one could worship God only in the way he prescribes—and that way, the apostle Paul explains, has *always* been through faith in the gospel. Even though Old Covenant believers did not understand the fullness of the gospel, they were worshipping God through it in the Passover and Sinai covenant! The "by grace alone and faith alone" gospel of the New Testament was nothing truly new—it was what God's prophets had *always* taught.

Paul and the apostles could still worship at the Jewish temple after Christ's resurrection without violating the gospel of faith or the second commandment because the synagogue, they understood, had always been established on the basis of the gospel. In so doing, they understood that the fulfillment of all the symbols was Christ. To worship in any other temple would be a violation of the second commandment, however, as you would be worshipping God other than in the way he prescribed.

Furthermore, Israel's history makes up Christianity's *present* identity. The New Testament presents Jesus as the New Israel, called up out of Egypt, tempted for 40 days in the wilderness, betrayed by his brothers, and sent into exile at his death. His resurrection was the fulfillment of the promises God gave of Jewish restoration from the exile.

Not only is Judaism part of Christianity's past, it is also integral to its future. Paul's epistles and the book of Revelation also speak of the future of the church in Jewish terms, and a completed, restored Israel is a major component of the future of Christ's work on earth. Ezekiel describes the future of the Messiah's people in terms of Jewish forms and temple customs.

In other words, Judaism is not just a chapter in Christianity's past, but a divine picture of Christ and, in that sense, the very gospel itself.

**The Qur'an is not the gospel.** In contrast, the Qur'an is *not* a perfect shadow that Jesus would fulfill. Parts of the Qur'an are tragically misleading. A "fulfilled Qur'an" would yield a drastically distorted Jesus! Taken as a whole, the Qur'an preaches a *different* gospel—at *no* point did Muhammad proclaim the gospel "by grace alone and faith alone," as did Moses, David, Abraham, and the other Old Testament prophets. *To say that Jesus fulfills the Qur'an downplays the central role the gospel plays in the Bible.*

Both Jesus and Paul insisted that Jews alone were given "the oracles of

God" and that "salvation was of the Jews" (Romans 9:4; John 4:22). The Qur'an, on the other hand, is not a divine covenant offered by God, nor is it a bearer of divine promises. Thus, it is not comparable to the Old Testament. It is in no way special revelation. Islam worships God *apart* from the ways he has directly commanded in the Old and New Covenants, and is thus a clear violation of the second commandment.

As I have noted throughout the book, there are elements of truth in the Qur'an. The Qur'an says some general and true things about God and repeats bits and pieces of the special revelation given to Jews and Christians. These can be helpful for pointing Muslims to the Bible, but that is not at all the same as saying that Islam is a divinely established forerunner of Jesus Christ.

It would be more accurate to compare believing Muslims to the converted Platonists of the first centuries AD than to "completed Jews." Platonists arguably had been prepared by God for the message of the gospel. Many terms from Platonic thought were employed in the worship and practice of Greek converts. Platonist converts did not remain in pagan temples, however, nor did they retain their identity in the Greek religions. They converted to Christianity.

That being said, it would be foolish for Christian missionaries *not* to use the Qur'anic admonitions to Muslims to study the "previous holy books" to their advantage.[9] If Paul could use even the Cretan philosophers when it served his purposes, certainly believers can use the Qur'an for theirs. We should be thankful for the elements of special revelation repeated in the Qur'an and use them whenever we can to point Muslims to the Bible.

### Biblical Problems

I find the biblical examples offered by "insider movements" to be unconvincing. It can hardly be said that Elisha gave Naaman God's go-ahead to worship him in pagan temples. The book of Daniel lauds Daniel, Shadrach, Meshach, and Abednego for refusing to bow to pagan gods and allows no implication that Shadrach, Meshach, and Abednego could have worshipped the golden statue as a symbol of God. How much easier would it have been for them to bow before Nebuchadnezzar, knowing that in their hearts they were "really bowing down to the real God" behind the statue? In Exodus 32 the children of Israel are rebuked for attempting to worship God "through" a golden calf!

Elisha's words to Naaman can, at most, only convey God's *forgiveness* for the wrong that Naaman would commit in weakness. Forgiveness, after all, implies sin, and to use God's grace in one situation to encourage sin as a general practice would be a blasphemous presumption. (Elisha's words, might, however, convey the mercy with which God looks upon an isolated C-6 convert who, overwhelmed with the weight of the world upon him, does not know what to do.) Examples of God's mercy are not a license for a programmed abrogation of the second commandment.

Jesus' words to the Samaritan woman in John 4 were about the true nature of worship, which is in spirit and truth. His words were not a license to worship in whatever temple one grew up in, but an invitation to move *beyond* the temple to him. Jesus' point was that true believers worshipped through *his body,* the new temple, in spirit and truth. Jesus' statement made temples obsolete. He further discouraged her from worshipping at the Samaritan temple by saying salvation was not found there, since "salvation is of the Jews." If any Samaritan went back and tried to access God through the Samaritan temple, he had clearly not understood what Jesus had explained. Jesus was not validating their religious system, *he was making it obsolete.*

Perhaps most importantly, we have *no example* in the book of Acts or Paul's epistles of a Christian convert remaining in a "pre-Christian" context to worship God, other than the earliest Christians continuing to worship occasionally at the synagogue. (And, as I noted above, the synagogue is clearly the exception, not the rule because the Jewish forms of worship embodied the gospels.) There were plenty of opportunities for Luke, the author of Acts, to tell us about pagans going back to "redeem" their temples, if this had been God's plan.

## Practical Problems

Phil Parshall has pointed out another major problem with the C-5 approach, and that is the integrity of the matter.[10] How will local Muslims feel when they find out that a Christian has converted to Islam solely for the purpose of leading them to embrace blatantly non-Muslim beliefs, such as substitutionary atonement and the Trinity? To put this in perspective, how would you feel if a Muslim moved into your community, "converted" to Christ, was baptized and joined your church, began to lead a Bible study...and began teaching in the Bible study that Muhammad was a superior prophet to Jesus? What emotional reaction would you have when you discovered this had been his purpose the entire time? How would you feel when you discovered that his "conversion" was really a strategy for *your* conversion? Parshall gives a number of examples where the C-5 approach has produced understandable hostility among Muslims who feel they have been deceived.

Parshall also notes that the C-5 approach has produced a disturbing number of doctrinally unsound Christians. In a case study involving one of the largest C-5 movements, Parshall notes that 96 percent of the converts *still* believed the Qur'an to be the inspired word of God, and 45 percent did not believe that God is a Trinity. C-5 advocates like to say they are a stream flowing toward C-4 Christians, but it appears they are, instead, a stagnant lake breeding dangerous confusion!

Another thing to consider is whether or not the C-5 approach removes one of the primary arenas in which God has historically demonstrated his power—a chance to show the superiority of Jesus above all other gods. The Scripture is replete with examples of Jehovah taking on rival claims to the universe's throne. Jehovah loves to show himself as the God who alone rules—superior to Pharaoh, the Canaanite gods, Goliath, Nebuchadnezzar, or Baal. His most effective witnesses (such as Moses, Joshua, David, Daniel, Elijah) literally provoked contests in which God could show his power above rival gods.

Moses declared that it was God's answering of prayer that would distinguish Jews from other peoples (Deuteronomy 4:7). Solomon said that all peoples would know that Jehovah is the Lord by the fact that he answered prayers prayed *at the Jewish temple*. Peter interpreted healing miracle of Acts 3 as God's desire to show the absolute distinctiveness of the gospel (Acts 4:12). God is determined to show his superiority to all rival gods through his willingness to answer prayers prayed in the name he has chosen and placed above every name, Jesus.

Doesn't the C-5 approach undermine God's strategy to glorify the name of Jesus by removing the distinction between the gospel and rival approaches to salvation? Would it not be better to stand on the distinctiveness of the gospel and trust God to show his great power, again, on behalf of the only name under heaven by which we must be saved?

## The Case for C-4

Seeing that C-5 lacks sufficient biblical and practical warrant, what about a C-4 approach? Can we use the Islamic names for Jesus, God, and the holy books without syncretizing the gospel?

It is my opinion that in most situations we can, and should do so.

J. Dudley Woodberry has demonstrated that almost all of the religious terminology of the Qur'an was used by Christians and Jews prior to Islam to refer to God.[11] *Allah* is simply Arabic for "the God," and long before Muhammad came along, that's the word Arabic Christians and Jews used to refer to God. Muhammad identified the God of whom he spoke as the God of Abraham and Moses. *Isa al-Masih* is only the Arabic translation of the Hebrew *Yeshua Meshach*.

The "Christian" versions of these names in Muslim culture often stem from Latin or Greek translations of the Hebrew. For example, in the Malay language, Christians refer to Jesus as "Yesus Kristus." This is not a translation from Hebrew into Malay, but from Hebrew into Greek into Latin, and then to Malay!

As I noted in chapter 4, you might ask, "But isn't the Islamic God so *different* from the Christian God that they properly cannot be called by the same name?" Again, believing wrong things about God and worshipping him incorrectly doesn't mean one is worshipping a *different* God. For example, Calvinists and Arminians believe very different things about the nature of the Christian God, yet who would say they are worshipping two different Gods? (For more on this point, I refer you back to the discussion on pages 58-60.)

You may also find it helpful to use traditionally Muslim styles and postures of worship in worshipping God. There is nothing sacrosanct about "traditionally Christian" tunes, prayer postures, or structure and times for worship services. The kingdom of God is not in external forms of worship, but in the change of heart found through faith in Christ. Churches in Muslim contexts may borrow significantly from the local customs, styles, and expressions of worship. Christian believers may, for example, find it best to worship on Friday,[12] take their shoes off as a show of respect when entering a place of worship, or pray with their faces to the floor. Taking one's shoes off signifies the same thing in Muslim culture that taking one's hat off often does in Western ones.

## Where Does All of This Leave Us?

Muhammad should not be called a prophet, and Christians should not see themselves as "completed Muslims." Islam fails the test of special revelation and should not be compared to such. The Qur'an does not teach the gospel. It should not be used as an authority in Christian practice or worship.

However, some aspects of Islam can be useful when recognized as part of God's *general* revelation. As we've seen throughout this book, Qur'anic verses and customs serve as signposts pointing Muslims *outside* of Islam to the special revelation given to the Jews. Islamic traditions are not fulfilled by Christ in the way Jewish ones are, but they can be used analogously to illuminate the gospel. We should point out how Christ fulfills the longings expressed in Islamic practices. Furthermore, Christians can and should take advantage of those places in the Qur'an that have repeated or referred to the biblical revelation.

---

> While doing all we can to make the gospel understandable to Muslims, we must not corrupt its message or dilute its distinctiveness.

---

We may choose not to refer to ourselves as "Christians" when asked what religion we are because of the baggage that word carries in the minds of Muslims. We may describe ourselves as "followers of Jesus Christ" using the Arabic name, *Isa al-Masih*. However, we should not, if pressed, deny that we are Christians and we should use that opportunity to explain the distinction between followers of Jesus and merely cultural Christians. We can never deny that Jesus is the Son of God, nor that we worship him as God. This is the essence of the Christian confession, and it is worth dying for. It is my opinion that we should never refer to ourselves as "Muslims," as this is too confusing for the Muslim, and it obscures the distinctiveness of our faith confession.

So, was my praying in the mosque an acceptable and helpful thing to do? I would say no. I think the confusion it caused was greater than any obstacles it removed.

The C-4 approach, generally speaking, seems to be the best application of contextualization among Muslims. It properly balances faithfulness to the gospel with redemption of the culture.

While doing all we can to make the gospel understandable to Muslims, we must not corrupt its message or dilute its distinctiveness. We should, like Paul, be "unashamed" of the gospel, because it really is the power of God to all those who believe...to the Jew first, and also to the Muslim.

# Notes

### Getting to the Issues of the Heart

1. Romans 1:18-21; Acts 17:23-27; Ecclesiastes 3:11.

2. For more information about Islam's growth in the U.S. and worldwide, see George Braswell, *Islam: Its Prophet, Peoples, Politics and Power* (Nashville, TN: Broadman & Holman Press, 1996).

### Chapter 1—Creating an Environment for Conversation

1. See, for example, John 1:13; 1 Corinthians 1:26-31; Ephesians 2:1-10.

2. Don Richardson, *Eternity in Their Hearts* (Ventura, CA: Regal Books, 1981), 23-4, 31-3.

3. An excellent discussion of what exactly all people "know" is J. Budziszewski's *What We Can't Not Know* (Dallas: Spence, 2003).

### Chapter 2—Understanding What Moves the Muslim

1. For a thorough explanation of many of the superstitions and customs, see Bill Musk's excellent duo of books, *Touching the Soul of Islam* (Grand Rapids, MI: Kregel, 2005) and *The Unseen Face of Islam* (Grand Rapids, MI: Kregel, 2004).

2. The recent work of Dr. Anthony Greenham, Professor of Islamic Studies at Southeastern Baptist Theological Seminary, confirms these three. Dr. Greenham conducted a qualitative study of the conversions of 22 Palestinian Muslim converts, 11 male and 11 female, and 10 male converts from Bangladesh. Greenham summarized,

   > Recurring themes are as follows: A prior crisis or felt need may precede conversion. Some individuals are disillusioned with Islam but others see Christ first in the pages of the Qur'an. They learn of Christ through various media, but the Bible is particularly important. Believers' teaching and love are crucial. Some have supernatural or mystical encounters, including dreams and miracles. Above all, Muslim converts encounter Christ himself. Calling out to him, they find forgiveness, love and assurance in the person of Jesus.

   Greenham says, "Jesus is always central...very few were converted because they rejected Islam." Anthony Greenham, "Muslim Conversions to Christ: An Investigation of Palestinian Converts Living in the Holy Land" (PhD diss., Southeastern Baptist Theological Seminary, 2004), xii-xiii.

3. Unless otherwise noted, the translation of the Qur'an used is Abdullah Yusuf Ali's classic *The Glorious Qur'an*, 3rd ed. (Lahore: Ashraf, 1938). Note that parentheses within the quotations indicate material added by the translator.

4. John 13:35; 1 John 4:8.

5. Greenham, xiii. See also note 2 above.

### Chapter 3—Understanding What Your Muslim Friend Believes

1. Emir Caner and Ergun Caner, *Unveiling Islam* (Grand Rapids, MI: Kregel, 2002), 122.

**Chapter 4—Misconceptions**

1. See www.erguncaner.com/home/debate/default.php. For further reading on this, see *Unveiling Islam,* written by former Turkish Muslims Emir and Ergun Caner.

2. Bukhari 2.24.541; 7.62.124; 8.76.456.

3. Sura 2:282; Bukhari 3.48.826. See also Emir Caner and Ergan Caner, *Unveiling Islam* (Grand Rapids, MI: Kregel, 2002), 43.

4. Sura 4:34.

5. Sura 2:223.

**Chapter 5—The Muslim Salvation Code**

1. The focus of the chapter will be on what is commonly believed among Muslims ("folk" religion), rather than on the official dogmas of orthodox Islam. Folk Muslims are those who have in some way deviated from the legalistic codes of formal Islam. Folk Islam arises out of the spiritual vacuum left by orthodox Islam and is influenced by the cultures preceding or surrounding existing Muslim communities. George Braswell says that folk Islam is "deviant, emphasizing local expressions and heartfelt needs over intellectual interests." Phil Parshall says that 70 percent of all Muslims fall into this category. See Braswell, *Islam: Its Prophet, People, Politics and Power* (Nashville, TN: Broadman & Holman Press, 1996), 74-76; and Parshall, *Bridges to Islam* (Carlisle, UK: Authentic Media, 2007), 16. Bill Musk's *The Unseen Face of Islam* and *Touching the Soul of Islam* (see "Getting to the Issues of the Heart," note 2) are studies of the needs that folk Islam reveals.

2. These similarities are due in no small measure to the fact Islam arose out of Judeo-Christian foundation. Islam's six essential beliefs are in one God, the Angels, the Books (the written records of God's revelation), the Apostles (or prophets), the Last Day, and the Decree (God's predestination over all things). See Sayyid Muhammad, *A Compendium of Muslim Theology and Jurisprudence,* tr. Saifuddin Annif-Doray (Sri Lanka: A.S. Nordeen, 1963), 3-15. J. Windrow Sweetman outlines some of the basic ideas behind Islamic soteriology in *Islam and Christian Theology,* pt. 1, vol. 2 (London: Lutterworth Press, 1947). Kenneth Cragg demonstrates how several aspects of Islamic soteriology can be utilized for Christian evangelization in "Islamic Theology: Limits and Bridges," in *The Gospel and Islam,* ed. Don McCurry (Monrovia: Missions Advanced Research & Communications, 1979), 196-208.

3. Muhammad Asad, "The Spirit in Islam," in *Islam—Its Meaning and Message,* ed. Khurshid Ahmad (Leicester: Islamic Foundation, 1993), 53.

4. "O my people, how is it that I bid you to salvation, but that you bid me to the Fire?"

5. Roland Muller, "The Muslim Doctrine of Salvation," *Bulletin of Christian Institutes of Islamic Studies* 3, nos. 1-4 (1980): 145.

6. See Abdullah Yusuf Ali's introduction to his classic translation and commentary on the Qur'an: *The Glorious Qur'an,* 8.

7. Ali, 6:164; 2:233. George Bebawi notes that some Islamic theologians have as many as 28 objections to the atonement. See "Atonement and Mercy: Islam between Athanasius and Anselm," in *Atonement Today: A Symposium at St. John's College,* ed. John Goldingay (London: S.P.C.K., 1995), 198.

8. Dr. Suleyman Derin, Ilahiyat Faculty, Marmara University, interview by author, January 26, 2003, in Istanbul, Turkey.

9. Gordon Nickel, "Islam and Salvation: Some On-Site Observations," *Directions,* Spring 1994 (23:1), 11.

10. Emir Caner and Ergun Caner, *Unveiling Islam* (Grand Rapids, MI: Kregel, 2002), 150.

11. Asad, 53.

12. Derin, 2003. When asked how it was fair for God to forgive sin without recompense, Derin responded, "In the hereafter, all those who have had something 'stolen' from them will be repaid in abundance." When asked how God would be repaid the honor and justice which was "stolen" from him by sin, Derin responded, "To ask such questions is to speak too anthropomorphically of God. Nothing can ever really be stolen from God in the sense as it is from a human. Since God needs nothing, nothing can be taken from him" (Derin, 2003).

13. Bill Bright's popular and effective packaging of the gospel for Western audiences. The Four Spiritual Laws are 1) "God loves you and has a wonderful plan for your life"; 2) "Sin has separated us from God"; 3) "Jesus Christ has paid the price for our sin, making the way to God open"; and 4) "We must individually receive Christ as our Savior."

14. Sura 7:8.

15. See Sweetman, 197-98.

16. Bakurah Shahiyyah, *The Torch of Guidance and the Mystery of Redemption,* tr. Sir William Muir (Edinburgh: T&T Clark, 1900), 21-22.

17. Bukhari 5.58.266 says,

> Then the Prophet came to us and I (addressing the dead body) said, "O Abu As-Sa'ib, may Allah's mercy be on you! I bear witness that Allah has honored you." On that the Prophet said, "How do you know that Allah has honored him?" I replied, "I do not know. May my father and my mother be sacrificed for you, O Allah's Apostle! But who else is worthy of it (if not Uthman)?" He said, "As to him, by Allah, death has overtaken him, and I hope the best for him. By Allah, though I am the Apostle of Allah, yet I do not know what Allah will do to me." By Allah, I will never assert the piety of anyone after him. That made me sad.

   A.S. Tritton tells of Muslims in history who have made similar statements in their dying moments, like al-Hajjaj, who said, "Would that God...when he put us in the world had made us independent of the next and delivered us from anxiety about what will save us from punishment" (A.S. Tritton, *Muslim Theology* [Bristol: Luzac & Company, 1947], 10). Tritton translates this from al-Jahiz, *Kitab al-Bayan wal-Tabyin* (1932), vol. 1, 145.

18. It should be noted that most Muslims believe every Muslim will eventually enter heaven so long as he has not committed *shirk*, the worship of another besides Allah. But many will have to pass through hellfire to be purified from their wickedness.

19. In fact, saying that God is present on earth "in the hearts of men" sounds like pantheism to many Sunnis, as it violates both the *tawhid* and the transcendence of Allah. "We do not say... that Allah is living with His creatures on Earth. We consider whoever says this is a non-believer or straying away because he attributed to Allah that which does not become Him" (Al-Uthaimin, *As-Sunnah Wal-Jammah,* 11).

20. Isma'il Raji al-Faruqi, *Tawhid: Its Implications for Thought and Life* (Herndon, VA: International Institute of Islamic Thought, 1991), 16. Al-Faruqi says that the Muslim life consists of seeing God as transcendent and absolutely one. Man observes God, hears his directives, and orders his life accordingly. Justification by faith is meaningless, he says, as it breaches the line between man and God. Man is to obey.

21. Derin, 2003.

22. Abdullah Yusuf Ali, the famous Muslim scholar who made one of the most respected English translations of the Qur'an, says that while the central character of the Bible is God and its chief aim is to lead men to know God, the central subject of the Qur'an is man, and its chief aim is to lead men to obey God (Ali, *Glorious Koran*, 8). Suleyman Derin says,

> Christianity is a very spiritual religion. It organizes the relationship between man and God. Islam organizes the relationship between man and man. Christianity's goal is for a man to know God, Islam's goal is for a man to properly serve God...Islam is a religion of practice. In Christianity what you believe is more important than what you do. Questions about where God is, what His essence is—these are irrelevant in Islam. Muslims are not allowed to argue about the nature of God. There is nothing on earth similar to which we can compare God. One day, man will see God. Until then, speculation about Him is useless.

Derin believes that much of Christian doctrine is the result of the mixing of Greek philosophy and Jewish belief, and that the apostle Paul is primarily to blame for this (Derin, 2003).

23. See Musk's *Touching the Soul of Islam* and *The Unseen Face of Islam* (see chapter 2, note 1).

24. Some have called al-Ghazali the "Thomas Aquinas of Islam," as he helped bring Aristotelian thought into Islamic doctrine. Perhaps more significantly, he was like Augustine in that many Islamic traditions claim him as a "father." Like Augustine, his theological contribution is characterized by its experiential depth about God, not just its intellectual brilliance. Suleyman Derin says that al-Ghazali taught the Muslim community to look at *sharia* through the eyes of a Sufi (Derin, 2003). A helpful chronicle of the history of Sufism is found in Parshall's *Bridges to Islam*, 23-52.

25. See, for example, Muhammad Ali, *A Manual of Hadith*, 1st American ed. (New York: Olive Branch Press, 1988), 40-67. "Purification" comprises the longest section in this collection.

26. See Sayyid Muhammad, 130-38.

27. Al-Uthaimin, *As-Sunnah Wal-Jammah*, 25.

28. There are many verses in the Qur'an which seem to forbid intercession. For example, the Qur'an says that there is no intercessor but Allah alone: "To God belongs exclusively the right of intercession" (39:44). The Qur'an, at times, implies that no one should look for help with his salvation from anyone else: "No bearer of burdens can bear the burden of another" (6:164; see also 2:45).

29. See also Qur'an 19:87.

30. Parshall, *Bridges to Islam*, 57.

## Chapter 6—Re-coding the Gospel

1. Nor would I want to downplay the centrality of penal substitution or the death of Christ in the gospel. Penal substitution is the essence of Christ's work on Calvary, and an indispensable part of the gospel! Christ gained victory over death and restored us to God precisely by dying, in weakness, *in our place,* thus propitiating (satisfying) the just wrath of the Almighty God by atoning for our sins with his blood. For more on this, see John Stott's classic, *The Cross of Christ* (Downers Grove, IL: InterVarsity, 2006).

2. Kenneth Cragg, "Islamic Theology: Limits and Bridges," in *The Gospel and Islam,* ed. Don McCurry (Monrovia: Missions Advanced Research & Communications, 1979), 203.

3. Of course, realize that Jesus' blood cleanses us, in part, by removing our guilt. First John 1:9 says that God is "faithful and *just* to *forgive* us our sins, and to *cleanse* us from all *unrighteousness.*"

Cleansing, forgiveness, and justification are ultimately all the same thing—rectifying the injustice of our sin is ultimately what cleanses us before God. The metaphor of cleansing, however, is tangible to Muslims, and it resonates with a need they encounter almost every day of their lives.

4. See Athanasius, *The Incarnation of the Word*, et al. George Bebawi notes, "Athanasius was more aware than Anselm of the link between creation, the grace of the divine image, the sin of Adam, and redemption." Bebawi, "Atonement and Mercy: Islam between Athanasius and Anselm," in *Atonement Today: A Symposium at St. John's College*, ed. John Goldingay (London: S.P.C.K., 1995), 198-99.

5. John of Damascus employed this line of reasoning, saying that it must be blasphemy to say the Qur'an was created (PG 96:1341).

6. John 1:14,18.

7. See "Timothy's Apology," in *Woodbroke Studies*, vol. 2, ed. A. Mingana (Cambridge: Heffer, 1928), 17, 20-24. See also Samuel Moffett, *A History of Christianity in Asia*, vol. 1 (Maryknoll: Orbis, 1998), 350.

8. Emir Caner and Ergun Caner, *Unveiling Islam* (Grand Rapids, MI: Kregel, 2002), 151.

9. N.T. Wright, *The Challenge of Jesus: Rediscovering Who Jesus Was and Is* (Downers Grove, IL: InterVarsity, 1999), 175-77.

10. Gustaf Aulén has demonstrated this in his *Christus Victor*. It is not necessary to agree with all of Aulén's conclusions to acknowledge that the resurrection was the predominant theme in the preaching of the Church Fathers.

11. Irenaeus, *Against Heresies* 3.18.7 (PG 7.1:937-38).

12. See discussion in Bill Musk, *Touching the Soul of Islam* (Grand Rapids, MI: Kregel, 2005), 186-87.

13. Philippians 2:5-11.

14. Isma'il Raji al-Faruqi, *Tawhid: Its Implications for Thought and Life* (Herndon, VA: International Institute of Islamic Thought, 1991), 4.

15. To learn how this approach has really taken off in Muslim countries around the world, see David Garrison's great book, *Church Planting Movements* (Richmond, VA: Wigtake Resources, 2003). Very exciting!

## Chapter 7—The Gospel Confronts the Ultimate Religion of Works

1. "The Meaning of Quran," in *The Glorious Qur'an*, translation and commentary by Abdullah Yusuf Ali, 8.

2. Galatians 2:14-17.

3. See, for example, Seyyed Hossein Nasr's acclaimed *The Heart of Islam: Enduring Values for Humanity* (San Francisco: HarperCollins, 2002). Nowhere in Nasr's robust description of Islam is there any counsel about having assurance of peace with God or safety in the afterlife.

## Chapter 8—The Objections, Part One

1. See "Additional Resources" for a compilation of sources that will deal more thoroughly with these and many other objections.

2. Norman Geisler and Abdul Saleeb, *Answering Islam* (Grand Rapids, MI: Baker, 2002), 269.

3. See John Calvin, *Institutes* 3.12-3.15 (LCC 20:754-97); Alister McGrath, *Iustitia Dei,* 3rd. ed. (Cambridge, UK: Cambridge University Press, 2005), vol. 1: 23-36; vol. 2: 39-53; Stott, *The Cross of Christ* (Downers Grove, IL: InterVarsity, 2006), 111-32; Leon Morris, *The Apostolic Preaching of the Cross* (Grand Rapids, MI: Eerdmans, 1998), 112-213; and Demarest, *The Cross and Salvation* (Wheaton, IL: Crossway Books, 2006), 171-82.

4. Muslims believe the main character in this story to be Ishmael, not Isaac. Though the fact that Isaac was the son in question is important in the overall development of the biblical story, it is not essential in seeing the redemptive picture the story presents. I found that it was best to not quibble with the Muslim over which son it was and, in telling the story, refer only to "Abraham's son" and not to Isaac directly.

5. See John 10:33,37-38.

### Chapter 9—The Objections, Part Two

1. Many Islamic scholars debate this point, claiming that the Christian Bible bears little resemblance to these three sacred books. The previous holy books had been forever lost, they claim, which is why Allah sent down the Qur'an to restore knowledge to the people. However, the majority of "ordinary" Muslims recognize the three holy books as the substance of the Christian Bible. Since this work has as its aim equipping the reader to deal with common Muslims, it will proceed on the assumption that the Muslim recognizes the Bible as the essence of the *Taurat, Zabur,* and *Injil.*

2. Somewhat ironically, there is substantial reason to believe that it is the Qur'an itself that has been changed. Recent research has demonstrated that after Muhammad, during the reign of Uthman, the third Muslim caliph (644-656), there were several different versions of the Qur'an being used. Uthman gave the order to canonize one version, the Medinan Codex, and to have the others rounded up and destroyed. See Norman Geisler and Abdul Saleeb, *Answering Islam*, 2nd ed. (Grand Rapids, MI: Baker, 2002), 197. See also Arthur Jeffery, *Islam: Muhammad and His Religion* (Indianapolis: Bobbs-Merrill, 1958), 7-8.

3. The Chester Beatty Papyri, c. AD 250, contain portions of the four Gospels. The Bodmer Papyri, c. AD 200, contain the Gospel of John and all of 1 and 2 Peter and Jude as they exist today; and the John Rylands fragment, which contains lines from John 18, dates from AD 138, at the latest. The vast majority of the New Testament is contained in the Vatican's Codex Vaticanus, which dates, at the latest, to AD 350. Hundreds of other manuscripts predate Muhammad. In addition, the Dead Sea Scrolls, which predate Christ, confirm that the Old Testament of Jesus' day was the same as in today's Bibles. See Geisler and Saleeb, 217-19.

4. For development of this argument, see Norman Geisler, *Baker Encyclopedia of Christian Apologetics,* "Muhammad, Alleged Miracles of" (Grand Rapids, MI: Baker, 1999), 509-14.

5. David Hume, *An Abstract of a Treatise on Human Nature,* 129-30.

### Chapter 10—The Challenge and the Hope

1. *Hudson Taylor's Spiritual Secret* (Chicago: Moody, 2009), ch. 11.

2. David Garrison, *Church Planting Movements* (Richmond, VA: Wigtake Resources, 2003).

3. Courtney Anderson, *To the Golden Shore: The Life of Adoniram Judson* (Grand Rapids, MI: Zondervan, 1956), 134.

4. John Piper, *Filling Up the Afflictions of Christ,* "How Few There Are Who Die So Hard," (Wheaton, IL: Crossway Books, 2009), 4.

5. *Regions Beyond,* vol. 37, no. 1, p. 2.

6. Patrick Johnstone, Jason Mandryk, eds., *Operation World* (Carlisle, UK: Paternoster, 2001), 462.

7. Barrett says, "The largest Christian force in Burma is the Burma Baptist Convention, which owes its origin to the pioneering activity of the American Baptist missionary Adoniram Judson." David Barrett, ed., *World Christian Encyclopedia* (New York: Oxford University Press, 1982), 202.

## Appendix—Speaking in Islamic Code

1. "The C1 to C6 Spectrum," *Evangelical Missions Quarterly* 34.4 (July 1998): 407-408.

2. I follow here the lead of Phil Parshall in his article, "Danger! New Directions in Contextualization," *Evangelical Missionary Quarterly* 34:4 (July 1998). See also the *International Journal of Frontier Missions* 17:1 (Spring 2000).

3. The term "outsider" refers to those cultural elements foreign to the surrounding Muslim culture. This can refer to language, styles of worship, and manners of expression. "Insider" refers to cultural elements natural and familiar to Muslims.

4. See the discussion on "The Jerusalem Council Applied: A Humble Appeal to C-5/Insider Muslim Ministry Movements to Consider Ten Questions" by Gary Corwin, Brother Yusuf, Rick Brown, Kevin Higgins, John Travis, and Rebecca Lewis, in the *International Journal of Frontier Missions* 24:1 (Winter 2007), 5-20, especially p. 7.

5. Acts 17:17.

6. See Philip Jenkins, *The Coming Christendom* (New York: Oxford Press, 2002), ch. 5.

7. For a helpful discussion of these examples that advocates of insider movements use, see Kevin Higgins, "The Key to Insider Movements: the 'Devoteds' in the Book of Acts," *International Journal of Frontier Missions* 21:4 (Winter 2004), 155-65.

8. Greeson's approach is outlined in *The Camel Method: How Muslims Are Coming to Faith in Christ!* (Lanforce, Inc., 2007). Greeson's 2007 edition of the Camel manual, however, makes a substantial movement toward a more C-4 approach, suggesting the Qur'an be used more as a starting point than an authority.

9. Admonitions such as the ones in 10:94 and 5:68-69,85 of the Qur'an to "consult the Book from before thee."

10. Parshall.

11. J. Dudley Woodberry, "To the Muslim I Became a Muslim?" *International Journal of Frontier Missions* 24:1 (Winter 2007), 23.

12. Some have argued that Sunday ought to be the regulated day for Christian worship, since the disciples worshipped on that first day of the week in remembrance of Jesus' resurrection. However, Paul's statement in Romans 14:5 that "some esteem one day as better than another; others esteem all days to be alike: each one should be fully convinced in his own mind" should caution us against insisting too strongly that there is only one appropriate day for Christian worship. Nowhere does the New Testament dictate that Christians must worship on Sunday, only that believers assemble regularly.

# The Truth About Islam Series
## John Ankerberg and Emir Caner

Emir Caner, converted Sunni Muslim and coauthor of the bestselling *Unveiling Islam*, grew up as the son of a devout mosque leader. He joins apologist John Ankerberg to provide this series of compact resources that will help you understand and interact with Muslims from an informed standpoint.

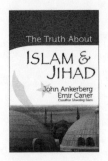

***The Truth About Islam and Jihad.*** Caner and Ankerberg take you to a new level of understanding about *jihad*, or "holy war," as they consider...

- the questionableness of calling Islam a "religion of peace"
- the Qur'an's contradictory teachings about conflict and tolerance
- the decisive radicalization of Muslims during the last quarter century
- the effects jihad may have upon twenty-first-century Christians

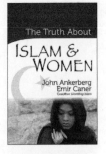

***The Truth About Islam and Women.*** Caner and Ankerberg help give you the real picture of women under Islam, including...

- the conditions of near-slavery women suffer in many Islamic cultures
- Muhammad's ambivalence toward females
- the contempt for women found in the Qur'an and the Muslim Traditions
- the dehumanizing double standard regarding men's and women's sexual behavior

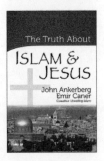

***The Truth About Islam and Jesus.*** Christians are often surprised to hear Muslims say, "We believe in Jesus too, and we hold him in great esteem." Are the Muslim Jesus and the Christian Jesus the same person? Caner and Ankerberg tackle key questions such as...

- What role does Jesus have in Islam?
- What do the Qur'an and the Traditions say about Him? What do they *not* say?
- Why are Muslims repulsed by the idea that Jesus is the divine Son of God?
- What practical results stem from belief in the Islamic Jesus?

# More Resources to Help You Understand and Reach Out

**Faith to Faith**
A Conversation About Christianity and World Religions
*Dan Scott*

Buddhists, Hindus, Muslims, Taoists…if your network of family, friends, neighbors, and co-workers doesn't include followers of other world religions, it probably will soon. Are you ready? How will you respond?

In this enlightening story about an interfaith symposium, nine engaging people—each representing a different religion—present their own spiritual views. In the "journal notes" that follow each presentation, you'll discover that as a Christian who is looking for truth, you have a lot in common with seekers in other religions. You'll see how to use those shared hopes and goals to build relationships and to talk honestly and lovingly about the important differences between the religions. You'll also see that God is continuing to reach out to all people through the gospel of Jesus Christ.

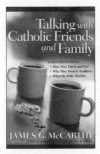

**Talking with Catholic Friends and Family**
Understanding How They Think and Feel, Why They Trust in Tradition, and What the Bible Teaches
*James G. McCarthy*

Here's a look into the way Catholics think about God, the Church, getting to heaven, and the practice of their religion. With a compassionate heart, James McCarthy shares real-life stories that contrast Catholicism with biblical Christianity and point the way to helping Catholics find a personal and saving relationship with Jesus Christ.

This book will equip you to talk openly and lovingly with Catholics in a clear and thought-provoking manner.

> *"Author James McCarthy has a unique gift for explaining complex issues in an uncomplicated way. I wholeheartedly recommend this book to anyone wishing to help seeking Catholics find Christ."*
>
> Vince O'Shaughnessy
> Former diocesan priest

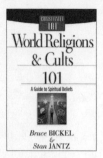

**World Religions and Cults 101**
A Guide to Spiritual Beliefs
*Bruce Bickel and Stan Jantz*

Investigate the world's major religions and cults in this comprehensive yet easy-to-understand guide. You'll discover how these spiritual beliefs got started, what they teach, and how they differ from biblical Christianity. Clear, concise explanations and respectful yet compelling comparisons and contrasts will make your exploration enjoyable and enlightening.

Reading lists for personal study as well as open-ended questions for group discussion or personal reflection make this the perfect resource for your look into world religions and cults.

To learn more about Harvest House books and
to read sample chapters, log on to our website:

**www.harvesthousepublishers.com**

HARVEST HOUSE PUBLISHERS
EUGENE, OREGON